They Teach That in College

College & Career Press
Chicago, Illinois

Project Staff

Managing Editor: Andrew Morkes

Additional Editorial Assistance: Amy McKenna, Jennifer Frisbie, Felicitas Cortez, Anne Paterson

Interior Design: The Glasoe Group

Cover Design: Meyers Design, Inc.

Proofreader: Jon Bieniek

Photo Credits

Front Cover (top left to right): University of Nevada-Las Vegas, IndexOpen, Eyewire Images

Back Cover (bottom): IndexOpen

Copyright © 2006 College & Career Press, LLC

ISBN 0-9745251-1-1

Published and distributed by

College & Career Press, LLC
5371 West Lawrence Avenue, #1
Chicago, IL 60630
773/248-6590
amorkes@chicagopa.com
www.collegeandcareerpress.com

Printed in the United States of America

For Kathy McKenna and Marion Morkes:
wonderful mothers who always encouraged their children
to follow their dreams—no matter their direction.

Table of Contents

Introduction

Business, Social Sciences/History, and Education are the most popular college majors today, but not every student has the interest or aptitude to be successful in these fields. Additionally, many of these fields are glutted with graduates who are forced to take lower-paying jobs or positions that are unrelated to their field of study.

They Teach That in College!? provides information about interesting, lucrative, and cutting-edge college majors unknown to many counselors, educators, and parents. It includes profiles of more than 75 college majors and schools, course listings, potential employers, contact information for colleges and universities that offer these programs, professional associations that offer career information about these fields, and interviews with educators in the field.

We hope that *They Teach That in College!?* becomes a valued and trusted resource as you navigate the challenges of college!

How This Book is Organized

They Teach That in College!? has 77 main chapters—68 of which focus on unique and interesting majors and nine of which focus on colleges and universities that are especially unique for reasons as varied as offering special instruction for students with learning disabilities (Beacon College and Landmark College), to offering one unique major (College of the Atlantic), to offering dozens of majors in one specific subject area (Unity College and Embry-Riddle Aeronautical University).

Now that we've explained what a unique college is, you might be asking yourself, 'What is a unique major?' We used two official criterion to select majors to include in this book: 1) the major had to be fast-growing and offer good employment and salary prospects for students, and 2) the major had to be offered at less than 25 percent of colleges and universities in the United States. A third unofficial criterion was that the major had to capture our imagination—in short it had to be fun and, hopefully, interesting to our readers.

The following paragraphs provide an overview of the specific subsections that are contained in the unique major and school chapters:

The unique major chapters have the following subsections: 1) an opening paragraph that details the major in question, classroom activities, and the typical educational path for students who pursue study in this field; 2) a list of typical courses that students will take if they study the major; 3) a list of potential employers of students who study the major; 4) a list of colleges and universities that offer the major (each entry includes contact information and the degree levels—such as certificate, associate, bachelor's, master's, and doctorate—that are available for the major; and, 5) a list of professional associations and organizations that you can contact for more information (job shadowing, free publications, financial aid, etc.) on the field.

The unique colleges and universities chapters have the following subsections: 1) an opening paragraph that details the school in question, including information on educational offerings and/or philosophy, financial aid, and extracurricular activities; 2) a list of majors that are offered; and, 3) contact information for the school in question.

Additionally, both types of articles occasionally feature interviews with college educators. These educators offer an overview of their programs, suggest high school classes that will help you prepare for college, present information on the future of their fields, and other useful advice. We would like to extend our sincere appreciation to the educators who contributed their time and expertise to this book.

In addition to the aforementioned sections, *They Teach That in College!?* also features a school index, a schools by state index, and an association/organization index.

Finally . . . Important Things to Keep in Mind
Remember that the world of education is constantly changing: majors may be renamed, available degree levels may change, programs may be dropped due to lack of funding, etc. Be sure to contact the school in which you are interested in attending for the latest program information.

Additionally, the Internet is also always changing. Websites are redesigned, new information is added . . . you get the idea. If you have trouble locating any of the websites listed in this book, try shortening the web address to its basic address. For example, if you are having trouble reaching the University of Delaware's art conservation website (http://www.udel.edu/artcons), shortening the address to the University's most basic address (e.g., http://www.udel.edu) will usually allow you to access the site and locate the information at the site's home page or by using its search feature.

Agricultural Education

Ask almost anyone to name typical agricultural careers, and you might hear "farmer" and "farm manager." While these careers remain very important to our food industry, today's agriculture and agricultural education involves much more than farming and managing farms. Agriculture students can now pursue dozens of majors that are far removed from planting crops and managing farms—majors as diverse as agricultural communications, finance, marketing, and sales; biochemistry; biological and food process engineering; food industry marketing and management; food manufacturing; international agronomy; landscape architecture; public horticulture; quantitative agricultural economics; turf science; and wood products manufacturing technology. Degrees available range from associate degrees to the doctorate.

Typical Courses:

> Varies by major

Potential Employers:

> Agricultural industry
> Food industry
> Broadcasting industry
> Financial industry
> Government agencies (e.g., U.S. Department of Agriculture)
> Virtually any other industry that specializes in agricultural-related products and services

Available At:

The following programs are just a sampling of the unique opportunities that are available to students interested in agricultural careers. Agricultural education programs are available at two- and four-year colleges and universities throughout the United States. Visit the websites of schools in your area to learn more about unique majors that are offered. You can also visit http://www.oneglobe.com/agriculture/agcolleg.html#usacol for a list of programs.

Cornell University
College of Agriculture and Life Sciences
177 Roberts Hall
Ithaca, NY 14853-4203
607/255-2036
http://www.cals.cornell.edu
Degrees available: Bachelor's degree, master's degree, doctorate
degree (26 agricultural majors are available)

University of Missouri
College of Agriculture, Food, and Natural Resources
Columbia, MO 65211
573/882-3846
cafnrweb@missouri.edu
http://cafnr.missouri.edu/Students/Majors/default.asp
Degrees available: Bachelor's degree, master's degree, doctorate
degree (15 agricultural majors are available)

Purdue University
School of Agriculture/Academic Programs in Agriculture
615 West State Street
West Lafayette, IN 47907-2053
765/494-8470
GOinAG@purdue.edu
http://www.agriculture.purdue.edu or
http://www.agriculture.purdue.edu/goinag/qanda.html
Degrees available: Associate degree, bachelor's degree (nearly 50
agricultural majors are available)

Texas A&M University
College of Agriculture and Life Sciences
109 Kleberg Building, 2402 TAMU
College Station, TX 77843-2402
979/845-4747
http://coals.tamu.edu
Degrees available: Bachelor's degree, master's degree, doctorate
degree (nearly 49 agricultural majors are available)

University of Wisconsin-Madison
College of Agricultural and Life Sciences
(Note: mailing address varies by agricultural department)
608/263-2400
http://www.wisc.edu/academics/majors.php
Degrees available: Bachelor's degree, master's degree, doctorate
degree (25 agricultural majors are available)

For More Information:

American Farm Bureau Federation
600 Maryland Avenue, SW, Suite 800
Washington, DC 20024
202/406-3600
http://www.fb.org

American Society of Agronomy
677 South Segoe Road
Madison, WI 53711
608/273-8080
http://www.agronomy.org

National FFA Organization
National FFA Center
PO Box 68960
Indianapolis, IN 46268-0960
317/802-6060
http://www.ffa.org

U.S. Department of Agriculture
1400 Independence Avenue, SW
Washington, DC 20250
202/720-2791
http://www.usda.gov

5

Interview: Dale Whittaker

The editors of *They Teach That in College!?* discussed the changing world of agriculture and agricultural education with Dale Whittaker, Associate Dean and Director of Academic Programs and Professor of Agricultural and Biological Engineering at Purdue University's College of Agriculture. Purdue offers nearly 50 undergraduate and preprofessional programs in agriculture.

Q. How has agriculture changed over the years?

A. After the green revolution/chemical revolution of post-World War II, agriculture became more mechanized and farmers were able to be more productive with the same amount of land. Over the past several decades, the focus has shifted from a production-oriented focus to a consumer-oriented focus. Today's agriculture is less about producing more with what we have and much more about producing the right products, getting them safely and cleanly packaged, and getting them to market and doing it in a sustainable way in a manner that the consumer desires. This focus has led to the rise of organic products, targeted health products, and more diversity in what is produced.

Q. How has agricultural education been affected by these changes?

A. In terms of agricultural education, there is much more of a focus on what the consumer wants, so there is more study in agricultural economics, international trade, entrepreneurship, engineering, processing, and packaging. A good example of this change in focus is in our agronomy program, where 50 percent of students are pursuing study in turf grass, sports field, lawn, and golf course management. The other 50 percent are interested in crop production.

Structural changes have also occurred in education. In the '50s and '60s, we had programs such as animal husbandry where students mainly took animal science classes. In the '70s, we started seeing more diversification in the curricula and selection of majors. At Purdue, that meant a larger selection of majors introduced. More recently, our students have focused on a very diverse curricula, with strong humanities, foreign languages, basic science, and areas of specialization. Today, our students are using more minors and double majors, and a much higher percentage are going on to graduate work.

Q. What are some of the most popular majors in Purdue's School of Agriculture?

A. Some of the majors that have experienced growth include food science, landscape architecture, landscape horticulture, turf grass management, pre-veterinary medicine, agricultural sales and marketing, wildlife, fisheries and aquatic sciences, and biological engineering. We have also had a very dramatic enrollment growth recently in biochemistry. And more students are becoming interested in companion animal management and the study of animals as models of human health.

Q. What nontraditional career options are available to agricultural majors?

A. Many of our students are pursuing careers in resource management. We have students who are managing fisheries in Alaska, students who are managing forests on the West Coast, and students who are managing professional football stadiums.

In terms of food science, many of the interesting new products, packaging, flavors, and prepared products are being developed by students with strong food science, as well as strong biology and chemistry, backgrounds. We also see a lot of our students going into medical school. A few are starting to go into law school. We see some students going into education. We have a core in our entomology major that teaches science education. We are also seeing a growing interest in forensic entomology (which uses the stages and development of insects to determine time and cause of death).

Some of our graduates also work for the government as regulators for the Environmental Protection Agency. Others go to work for companies and write impact statements and permitting statements for these regulators. So, we have students regulating other students. A small number of our graduates are farming. About 7 percent go on to manage family farms or large corporate farms. And corporate farming is an international career; these students find jobs all over the world.

Q. What does the future hold for agricultural education?

A. Agricultural education will continue to move toward a consumer-driven focus. The next educational focus in agriculture will be on human health. That's really where food science, biochemistry, and the animal sciences have gone. Even in our natural resources department, one of the fastest-growing programs is humans in the environment and managing natural and urban landscapes. I also think we will continue to see the basic sciences, such as plant science, molecular science, proteomics, ionomics, and genomics, move into the undergraduate curriculum.

American College of the Building Arts

The American College of the Building Arts is the only college in the United States to offer a baccalaureate program in the building arts. Founded in 2005, the College offers degrees in the six traditional building trades (see list below). While teaching traditional building methods, the College stresses that it is "committed to teach . . . the most up-to-date methods of quality fabrication and building technology" in order to prepare students for success in the work world. Students will learn about these trades via hands-on workshops (about 50 percent of instructional time), lectures, discussions, field trips, and demonstrations by master craftworkers. More than 8.3 million people are employed in the U.S. construction industry, according to the U.S. Department of Labor. The construction industry is one of the largest industries in the United States.

8

Available Fields of Study:

Students at the College can pursue associate and bachelor's degrees in one of the six traditional building trades:
> Architectural Stone
> Carpentry
> Masonry
> Ornamental Ironwork
> Plasterwork
> Timber Framing

For More Information:

American College of the Building Arts
21 Magazine Street
Charleston, SC 29401
877/283-5245
info@buildingartscollege.us
http://www.buildingartscollege.us
Degrees available: Associate degree, bachelor's degree

Art Conservation

Imagine the *Mona Lisa* marred by soot, smoke, and water damage as a result of a fire. A Civil War-era photograph disintegrating with age. Or just the vibrant colors of a beloved family painting dulled by time. The world would be a far less beautiful and interesting place without art. Art conservators protect paintings, photographs, sculpture, works of art on paper, textiles, architecture, books, ethnographic and archaeological objects, and other types of artwork from damage inflicted by temperature and humidity extremes, excessive light, pests, pollutants, poor handling practices, natural disasters, and accidental damage. They work to prevent damage to at-risk objects and attempt to conserve artwork that has been damaged. A master's degree in art conservation is required to work in this field.

Typical Courses:

> Art Conservation
> Techniques of Examination and Documentatation
> Conservation Science: Properties and Behavior of Materials
> Structure of Works of Art
> Methods of Analysis
> Technology and Conservation of Paintings
> Professionalism in Conservation

Potential Employers:

> Museums
> Conservation centers
> Private collectors
> Art and antique dealers
> Government agencies
> Galleries
> Auction houses

Available At:

University of California-Los Angeles
Conservation of Archaeological and Ethnographic Materials Program
A410 Fowler Building, Box 951510
Los Angeles, CA 90095-1510

310/794-4837
dascott@ucla.edu
http://ioa.ucla.edu/conservation
Degrees available: Master's degree

University of Delaware
Winterthur/University of Delaware Program in Art Conservation
303 Old College
University of Delaware
Newark, DE 19716-2515
302/831-3489
art-conservation@udel.edu
http://www.udel.edu/artcons
Degrees available: Bachelor's degree, master's degree, doctorate
degree

New York University
Conservation Center of the Institute of Fine Arts
212/992-5848
conservation.program@nyu.edu
http://www.nyu.edu/gsas/dept/fineart/ifa/curriculum/
conservation.htm
Degrees available: Master's degree

State University College of New York-Buffalo
230 Rockwell Hall, 1300 Elmwood Avenue
Buffalo, NY 14222
716/878-5025
http://www.buffalostate.edu/gradprog.xml?bpid=133
Degrees available: Master's degree

University of Texas-Austin
1 University Station
D7000
Austin, TX 78712

Fun Fact

Recommended undergraduate classes, according to the
American Institute for Conservation of Historic and Artistic
Works, include science, the humanities (art history, anthropology, and archaeology), and studio art.

512/471-3821
http://www.gslis.utexas.edu/programs/certificates/conservation.php
Degrees available: Master's degree (combined with a certificate
in the Conservation of Library and Archival Materials or a certificate in the Preservation Administration of Library and
Archival Materials)

For More Information:

**American Institute for Conservation
of Historic and Artistic Works**
1717 K Street, NW, Suite 200
Washington, DC 20036-5346
202/452-9545
info@aic-faic.org
http://aic.stanford.edu

Art Therapy

Artists have been using creative self-expression as an outlet to express their feelings and emotions since the beginning of time. But you don't have to be a famous painter or sculptor to understand the basic premise behind the discipline of art therapy—expressing oneself can be an emotional, healing, and therapeutic process. Art therapy is a health profession that is built upon this fundamental principle that the creative process can enhance a person's physical, mental, and emotional well-being. The art therapist serves as the facilitator in guiding a client through the process of resolving conflicts and problems, developing interpersonal skills, reducing stress, increasing self-esteem, and coming to a sense of self-understanding—by means of personal artistic expression. People who enter the field have a strong commitment to working with people in one-on-one situations. They believe in the nurturing and healing power of art and its importance in helping people resolve personal issues resulting from a variety of life challenges such as physical or mental illness, grief, or trauma. A master's degree in art therapy is required for professional certification in art therapy. Students entering master's programs may have undergraduate degrees in areas such as art, education, or psychology.

Typical Courses:

> Theories of Art Therapy, Counseling, and Psychotherapy
> Ethics and Standards of Practice
> Assessment and Evaluation
> Individual, Group, and Family Techniques
> Human and Creative Development
> Research Methods
> Drawing
> Painting
> Sculpting
> Clinical Practice: Counseling Skills in Art Therapy Practice

Did You Know?

Art therapists earn annual median salaries of approximately $42,000, according to the American Art Therapy Association.

Potential Employers:

> Hospitals (medical and psychiatric)
> Clinics

12

> Public and community agencies
> Wellness centers
> Educational institutions
> Businesses
> Private practices
> Outpatient counseling clinics
> Residential treatment facilities
> Halfway houses
> Prisons
> Domestic violence and homeless shelters
> Correctional facilities
> Nursing homes
> Hospice programs

Available At:

The following list of schools offering programs in art therapy is not exhaustive. For a complete list of programs that are approved by the American Art Therapy Association, visit http://www.arttherapy.org/staep.html.

School of the Art Institute of Chicago
Sharp Building, Room 35, 4th Floor Annex
37 South Wabash Avenue
Chicago, IL
312/899-7481
arttherapy@artic.edu
Degrees available: Master's degree

Emporia State University
Department of Psychology and Special Education
Campus Box 4031
1200 Commercial Street
Emporia, KS 66801-5087
http://www.emporia.edu/acadaff/arther.htm
Degrees available: Master's degree

University of Louisville
College of Education and Human Development
Expressive Therapies, Room 320
Louisville, KY 40292
etemail@louisville.edu
http://www.louisville.edu/edu/ecpy/et/ArtThx.htm
Degrees available: Master's degree

Marylhurst University
Graduate Program in Art Therapy
17600 Pacific Highway (Highway 43), PO Box 261
Marylhurst, OR 97036-0261
503/636-8141
studentinfo@marylhurst.edu
http://www.marylhurst.edu/search/index.html
Degrees available: Master's degree

Marywood University
Department of Art
2300 Adams Avenue
Scranton, PA 18509-1598
570/348-6278
parkerbell@es.marywood.edu
http://www.marywood.edu/departments/art/grad/grad.html#at
Degrees available: Master's degree

Mount Mary College
2900 North Menomonee River Parkway
Milwaukee, WI 53222-4597
414/258-4810, ext. 301
http://www.mtmary.edu/at.htm and http://www.mtmary.edu/
arttherapy.htm
Degrees available: Bachelor's degree, master's degree

New York University
34 Stuyvesant Street
New York, NY 10003
212/998-5726
ia4@nyu.edu
http://education.nyu.edu/depts/art/programs/5
Degrees available: Master's degree

Southern Illinois University-Edwardsville
Department of Art and Design
PO Box 1046
Edwardsville, IL 62026
618/650-2000
jgausep@siue.edu
http://www.siue.edu/ART/areas/art_therapy
Degrees available: Master's degree

14

Southwestern College
PO Box 4788
Santa Fe, NM 87502-4788
877/471-5756
admissions@swc.edu
http://www.swc.edu/programs/MA_art_therapy.htm
Degrees available: Master's degree

Ursuline College
Art Therapy Department
2550 Lander Road
Pepper Pike, OH 44124
440/646-8139
gradsch@ursuline.edu
http://www.ursuline.edu/acadaff/art_therapy/masters.htm
Degrees available: Master's degree

For More Information:

American Art Therapy Association
1202 Allanson Road
Mundelein, IL 60060-3808
888/290-0878
info@arttherapy.org
http://www.arttherapy.org

National Coalition of Arts Therapies Associations
8455 Colesville Road, Suite 1000
Silver Spring, MD 20910
http://www.ncata.org

Interview: Bruce Moon

Dr. Bruce Moon is the Graduate Program Director of the Art Therapy Department at Mount Mary College in Milwaukee, Wisconsin. He discussed his program and the education of art therapy students with the editors of *They Teach That in College!?*

Q. Please provide a brief overview of your program.

A. Art therapy is a challenging and exciting career choice that allows individuals to combine skills in art making with the desire to help persons who are suffering with emotional, physical, or developmental challenges. At Mount Mary College the art therapy program is housed in the Art and Design Division and is a vital and dynamic component of graduate education.

Our approach to art therapy education is uniquely art-based and experiential, and we endeavor to provide a creative integration of artistic, academic, and clinical education. In every way possible we attempt to live-out our program mission, "Art Therapy: Compassion in Action."

The Graduate Art Therapy Program utilizes an art-based and experiential approach to graduate level art therapy education. The faculty and students strive to create a community of learners in which all members share a commitment to meaningful participation in graduate level academic, artistic, clinical, and intra- and inter-personal study.

Classes are offered at times designed to accommodate students' needs. Students may choose from among daytime, evening, and weekend classes. The course of study combines disciplined artistic inquiry with intensive academic investigation of art therapy and counseling theories and techniques, and hands-on clinical practicums and supervision. These elements provide students with a thorough and rich educational experience.

In addition to our nationally known full-time faculty, part-time faculty members who are actively working in the field enrich the program. Each semester, guest lecturers—national leaders and innovators of the profession—contribute diversity to the program with exciting, current topics in art therapy that broaden and enrich the students' perspectives. Small group, experiential, and art-based learning is a key strength of the program. Students have the opportunity to select from a wide range of practicums through which they develop their skills in real-life treatment settings.

Q. What high school subjects should students focus on to be successful in this major?

A. It is important to note that art therapy is a master's degree level of entry profession. High school students can begin to prepare for their undergraduate work and later graduate education by taking the maximum number of studio art classes and psychology/social science classes. It is also important to develop good writing skills and to become well versed in metaphoric language. English composition and literature courses, in addition to art and psychology courses, help to prepare students for the rigors of undergraduate and graduate study.

Q. What are the most important personal and professional qualities for art therapy (AT) majors?

A. I believe that the most important personal and professional qualities for art therapy students are twofold: 1) a genuine love of art making, and 2) a deep commitment to humanity and a longing to make the world a better place. Of course it is important also to have some measure of artistic skill, a capacity to articulate ideas in a coherent manner, and the discipline to succeed as an art therapy scholar and practitioner.

Q. What advice would you offer AT majors as they graduate and look for jobs?

A. It is often important for art therapists to have an entrepreneurial spirit and to be willing to sell themselves to potential employers. Art therapy is a unique and potent treatment modality, but it is a little less well known than some other helping professions. It helps to be able to confidentially and clearly describe the profession to potential employers and to be able to make a strong case for why art therapy is needed in a particular setting.

I also always advise graduates to not let the ideal be the enemy of the good. By that I mean there are few 'perfect' jobs out in the world, and sometimes it is important to just get your foot in the door so that they can prove their worth.

Q. How will the field of art therapy change in the future?

A. I've been in the profession for more than 30 years now, and the field of art therapy has made many changes in that time. Many years ago the majority of art therapists worked in psychiatric hospitals. Today, however, the field has expanded to include art therapists in nursing homes, prisons, schools, community counseling agencies, hospice programs, rehabilitation hospitals, oncology units, and residential treatment facilities. I suspect that over the next 10 to 20 years ever more new applications of art therapy will emerge.

Another significant change will come about as more states codify licensure procedures for art therapists, which will result in art therapists routinely receiving third party payment for their services. All things considered, this is an exciting time to consider entering the profession of art therapy.

Automobile Engineering Technology

If you have a passion for cars, and an aptitude for engineering, a degree in automotive engineering technology might be right up your alley. While your in-class work will focus on design, development, and testing of all kinds of motorized vehicles, most programs will also require a significant amount of time getting practical, hands-on experience in a variety of settings. Of the career paths available to automotive engineers, all require an interactive, people-focused personality—you'll be working daily with customers and personnel from other departments. Careers in automotive engineering are plentiful; most graduates find jobs with major automotive manufacturers.

Typical Courses:

> Calculus
> Statistics
> DC Circuits
> Computer-Aided Drafting
> Material Processing and Metallurgy
> Automotive Drivability and Diagnosis
> Fluid Power Systems
> Automotive Thermodynamics and Engine Design
> Industrial and Construction Safety
> Automotive Technology and Systems

Potential Employers:

> Automotive manufacturers
> Engineering firms

Available At:

Lawrence Technological University
College of Engineering
21000 West Ten Mile Road
Southfield, MI 48075-1058
248/204-2563
http://www.ltu.edu/engineering/mechanical/
engineering_mechanical__master_3.asp
Degrees available: Master's degree

Fun Fact

There were 21,640 dealerships selling new cars in the United States in 2005, according to the National Automobile Dealers Association.

University of Michigan
Department of Engineering
273B Chrysler Center, 2121 Bonisteel Boulevard
Ann Arbor, MI 48109-2092
734/763-1134
autoeng@umich.edu
http://interpro.engin.umich.edu/auto
Degrees available: Bachelor's degree

Minnesota State University
Department of Automotive and Manufacturing Engineering Technology
205 Trafton Science Center E
Mankato, MN 56001
507/389-6383
http://www.cset.mnsu.edu/aet/newstudents/generalinfo.htm
Degrees available: Bachelor's degree

For More Information:

American Society for Engineering Education
1818 N Street, NW, Suite 600
Washington, DC 20036-2479
202/331-3500
http://www.asee.org

Junior Engineering Technical Society, Inc.
1420 King Street, Suite 405
Alexandria, VA 22314
703/548-5387
info@jets.org
http://www.jets.org

Aviation Management

Aviation management prepares students to work in the airline industry in management, marketing, finance, sales, personnel, public relations, and other related areas. Programs can often have different areas of emphasis, based on the department in which they are housed. Some programs are designed for students interested in a curriculum containing a strong engineering science and analysis component, while others are for those who prefer a liberal arts background and a broader base of social sciences or business management principles. Some programs require actual flight training, while others do not. Degrees are available at all academic levels.

Typical Courses:

> Introduction to Aviation Management
> National Airspace Systems
> Air Traffic Control
> Aviation Law
> Airport Planning
> Airport Management
> Airline Management
> Airline Marketing
> General Aviation Operations
> Aviation Industry Regulation
> Aviation Management Writing and Communication
> Aviation Management Practices and Processes
> Air Transport Labor Relations
> Fiscal Aspects of Aviation Management
> Aviation Industry Career Development

Fun Fact

According to the Federal Aviation Administration, there are a total of 19,576 airports in the United States—of which 510 are Commercial Service.

Potential Employers:

> Airlines
> Commercial service airports (e.g., Chicago O'Hare International, Detroit Metro, and Los Angeles International)
> General aviation and reliever airports (e.g., Teterboro Airport, New Jersey, or DuPage Airport, Illinois)
> Federal Aviation Administration
> Transportation Security Administration
> Aviation/aerospace manufacturers (e.g., Lockheed-Martin, B. F. Goodrich Aerospace, Bell Helicopters-Textron, and The Boeing Company)
> General aviation companies (e.g., Cessna Aircraft Company, Signature Flight Support)

Available At:

The following list of aviation management programs is not exhaustive. Check with academic institutions near you to determine if majors, minors, or concentrations are available in aviation management.

Eastern Michigan University
Aviation Management Technology Program
School of Technology Studies
122 Sill Hall
Ypsilanti, MI 48197
734/487-1161
http://www.emich.edu/sts/aviation_management.htm
Degrees available: Bachelor's degree

Embry-Riddle Aeronautical University
Daytona Beach Campus
600 South Clyde Morris Boulevard
Daytona Beach, FL 32114-3900
386/226-6000
http://www.erau.edu/db/degrees/b-aviationmgt.html
Degrees available: Bachelor's degree, master's degree

Miami Dade College (multiple campuses)
https://sisvsr.mdc.edu/ps/sheet.aspx
Degrees available: Associate degree

The Ohio State University
Department of Aviation
164 West 19th Avenue

Columbus, OH 43210
614/292-2405
aviation@osu.edu
http://aviation.osu.edu/considering_aviation/
degree_aviationmanage.php
Degrees available: Bachelor's degree

St. Cloud State University
Department of Aviation
720 Fourth Avenue South, 216 Headley Hall
Saint Cloud, MN 56301-4498
320/308-2107
aviation@stcloudstate.edu
http://www.stcloudstate.edu/aviation
Degrees available: Bachelor's degree

Southern Illinois University Carbondale
Department of Aviation Management and Flight
Mailcode 6623
Carbondale, IL 62901-6623
618/453-8898
http://www.aviation.siu.edu
Degrees available: Bachelor's degree, master's degree

23

Western Michigan University
College of Aviation
237 North Helmer Road
Battle Creek, MI 49015
269/964-6375
aviation_advising@wmich.edu
http://www.wmich.edu/aviation/programs/administration.htm
Degrees available: Bachelor's degree

For More Information:

Air Transport Association of America
1301 Pennsylvania Avenue, NW, Suite 1100
Washington, DC 20004-1707
202/626-4000
ata@airlines.org
http://www.airlines.org

Federal Aviation Administration
800 Independence Avenue, SW, Room 810
Washington, DC 20591
202/366-4000
http://www.faa.gov

Interview: David NewMyer

Dr. David NewMyer, Professor and Chair of Aviation Management and Flight at Southern Illinois University Carbondale, discussed his program and the education of aviation management students with the editors of *They Teach That in College!?*

Q. Please provide an overview of your program.

A. The Bachelor of Science in Aviation Management program offered at Southern Illinois University Carbondale is a 48-semester-hour major consisting of the following:

1. A 12 semester hour set of core aviation management classes including such individual courses as Aviation Management Writing and Communication, Aviation Management Practices and Processes, Air Transport Labor Relations, Fiscal Aspects of Aviation Management, and Aviation Industry Career Development. A student enrolled in the Aviation Management program is required to take four of these five courses.

2. A 15-semester-hour set of Aviation Management major classes including Introduction to Aviation Management, Air Traffic Control, Airport Planning, Aviation Industry Regulation, Airport Management, Airline Management, General Aviation Operations, Legal Aspects of Aviation, Aviation Maintenance Management, Aviation Safety Management, National Airspace Systems and Aircraft Product Support Management. A student in the program must take five of these classes.

3. A nine-hour set of Aviation Management electives taken from the above list of classes or from a selected list of elective classes from other departments including psychology, marketing, information management systems, and many more.

4. A 12-hour set of internship, cooperative education, independent study, or approved equivalent classes.

A student in this major must also have either a technical background upon entry or must fulfill a 31-semester-hour approved career elective requirement that relates to the student's career objectives to enter a segment of the aviation industry.

Finally, a student in this major must complete a 41-semester-hour university core curriculum that includes mathematcomposition, public speaking, science, social science, humanities, fine arts, PE/health, and multicultural and interdisciplinary classes.

Students graduating with this major go on to work to all parts of the aviation industry: manufacturing, airlines, general aviation, government (including airports), and the military. Key job titles held by alumni include business operations professional, cost estimator, technical writer, aircraft product support specialist, facilities programmer, pilot/flight officer, aviation maintenance manager, on-board crew specialist, crew scheduler, dispatcher, ramp manager, customer service manager, airport manager, airport operations specialist, airport marketing representative, air traffic control specialist, general manager, director of corporate aviation, flight department manager, chief pilot, vice president (in several locations in the industry), and many more.

25

Q. What high school subjects/activities should students focus on to be successful in this major?

A. In high school, I would recommend that students focus on the basics such as mathematics, English, science, social science, and computing/technology skills. It is very important that all students entering a college or university program have very good writing and communication skills and can easily speak in front of an audience (large or small). Also, knowing about teamwork and leadership skills in a team environment are excellent skills to have. So, working in student government, in student clubs or organizations, and in athletics are all good for learning those things. Finally, computational and technology skills (working with computer hardware and software) are important.

Q. What are the most important personal and professional qualities for aviation management majors?

A. ✓ Be a people person (good interpersonal skills)
✓ Be able and willing to learn

✓ Have an enthusiastic, positive, and outgoing attitude
✓ Look to the future and not the past
✓ Don't be a complainer, be a 'doer'
✓ Be a hard worker

Q. How will the field of aviation management change in the future?

A. The field of aviation management will change with the aviation industry as a whole. For example, one must follow aircraft technology trends (the Airbus A-380 and the Boeing 787 'Dreamliner'), the Very Light Jet phenomenon, and the explosion in the number of regional jets over the last decade. Also, one must follow what is going on operationally in the aviation industry; there have been many mergers of aerospace manufacturers, airlines, and general aviation companies over the past two decades. Also, low-cost carriers such as Southwest Airlines, jetBlue Airways, AirTran Airways, and Frontier Airlines are changing how airlines are managed and operated. Finally, airports are expanding tremendously . . . consider the multi-billion dollar expansion underway at St. Louis Lambert International and the one just approved for Chicago O'Hare International. All of these changes create opportunities for future aviation management majors. Future aviation management students wanting to know more should consult the latest Federal Aviation Administration (FAA) Aerospace Forecast at the FAA website: http://www.faa.gov.

Bagpiping

Carnegie Mellon University in Pittsburgh, Pennsylvania, is the only school in the United States that offers a degree in bagpiping. The degree is offered as part of the University's instrumental curriculum in the School of Music. As part of this curriculum, bagpipe majors take lessons on the bagpipe, play in the university pipe band, and take a series of theoretical bagpipe classes (see the list below). Interested students should first apply to Carnegie Mellon through the school's undergraduate admissions office. They then complete an audition application for the School of Music, and undergo an audition. Students who complete the program receive a bachelor of fine arts degree in music performance (bagpipe).

Typical Courses:

> Bagpipe Composers
> Bagpipe Construction
> Bagpipe Literature and Repertoire
> Bagpipe Maintenance
> Bagpipe Reedmaking
> Bagpipe Theory
> Bagpipe Advanced History
> Bagpipe Advanced Literature and Repertoire

Potential Employers:

> Musical groups
> Bands
> Freelance
> Cultural organizations

Did You Know?

The bagpipe is the national instrument of Scotland.

Available At:

Carnegie Mellon University
School of Music
Office of Recruitment and Enrollment
music_admissions@andrew.cmu.edu
http://music.web.cmu.edu
Degrees available: Bachelor's degree

For More Information:

National Association of Schools of Music
11250 Roger Bacon Drive, Suite 21
Reston, VA 20190-5248
703/437-0700
info@arts-accredit.org
http://nasm.arts-accredit.org

Bagpipe Web Directory
http://www.bobdunsire.com/bagpipeweb

Beacon College

Beacon College serves students with language-based learning disabilities, auditory and visual processing differences, reading/writing disabilities, expressive/receptive language deficits, math disabilities, and ADD/HD. It is the only accredited college in the United States with a program exclusively for students with learning disabilities that offers a bachelor of arts degree. Students can choose to earn an associate of arts degree or a bachelor of arts degree in human services, liberal studies, or computer information systems. The College strives to provide every student with the tools and support they need to succeed in school, and features a strong Educational Support Services program. Other programs include the Field Placement Program, which allows students to gain valuable work experience in their chosen field while still in school; and the Cultural Studies Abroad Program, which offers students the option to study abroad in several countries. Students have previously taken advantage of this program to visit England, France, Germany, Ireland, Italy, Spain, and Switzerland. The school has several clubs and student organizations, such as the Book Club, Poets and Writers Club, and Fishing Club.

Available Fields of Study:

> Human Services
> Liberal Studies
> Computer Information Systems

For More Information:

Beacon College
105 East Main Street
Leesburg, FL 34748
352/787-7660
http://www.beaconcollege.edu
Degrees available: Associate degree, bachelor's degree

Bioinformatics

If you are interested in computer science and biology, then the new field of bioinformatics might be for you. Bioinformatics can be generally described as the application of cutting-edge computer science to analyze and manage biological information. Bioinformatics played a significant role in the Human Genome Project, and it has also helped shorten the research and development time for pharmaceuticals. Experts predict that bioinformatics will be used in the future to create designer drugs and treatments that will be much more effective for individual patients. Degrees in bioinformatics, sometimes known as biostatistics, are available at all levels, but advanced degrees are typically required for the best positions in the field.

Typical Courses:

> Fundamentals of Biology
> Genetics
> Cell and Molecular Biology
> Biochemistry
> Bioinformatics
> Bioethics
> Computer Science
> Database Design
> Fundamentals of Chemistry
> Organic Chemistry
> Calculus
> Statistics
> Data Structures
> Discrete Mathematics
> Algorithms

Potential Employers:

> Pharmaceutical companies (such as Aventis, Bristol-Myers Squibb, Merck & Co., Pfizer, and Wyeth)
> Research laboratories
> Colleges and universities
> Government agencies
> Software companies

Available At:

Only a few colleges offer associate and bachelor's degrees in bioinformatics. For a list of colleges that offer graduate degrees in bioinformatics, visit http://www.colorado.edu/chemistry/bioinfo.

Boston University
44 Cummington Street
Boston, MA 02215
617/358-0752
bioinfo@bu.edu
http://www.bu.edu/bioinformatics
Degrees available: Master's degree, doctorate degree

University of California-Santa Cruz
Department of Biomolecular Engineering
1156 High Street
Santa Cruz, CA 95064
831/459-2158
http://www.soe.ucsc.edu/programs/bioinformatics
Degrees available: Bachelor's degree, master's degree, doctorate degree

Canisius College
Department of Bioinformatics
2001 Main Street
Buffalo, NY 14208-1098
716/888-2430
http://www.canisius.edu/bif
Degrees available: Bachelor's degree

University of Colorado
Department of Preventive Medicine and Biometrics
4200 East 9th Avenue
Campus Box B119
Denver, CO 80262
303/315-9030
http://pmb.uchsc.edu/biostatistics/index.html
Degrees available: Master's degree, doctorate degree

Howard Community College
10901 Little Patuxent Parkway, ILB 239
Columbia, MD 21044
410/772-4441
http://www.howardcc.edu/business/BioinformaticsAADegree.htm
Degrees available: Associate degree

University of Idaho
Department of Biological Sciences
PO Box 443051
Moscow, ID 83844-3051
208/885-6280
http://www.sci.uidaho.edu/biosci/BCB
Degrees available: Master's degree, doctorate degree

Indiana University
School of Informatics
Informatics and Communications Technology Complex
535 West Michigan Street, Room 475
Indianapolis, IN 46202-3103
317/278-7602
info@informatics.iupui.edu
http://informatics.iupui.edu
Degrees available: Bachelor's degree, master's degree

University of Minnesota
School of Public Health
MMC 819
420 Delaware Street, SE
Minneapolis, MN 55455
612/626-3500
sph-ssc@umn.edu
http://www.catalogs.umn.edu/grad/programs/g021.html
Degrees available: Master's degree, doctorate degree

State University of New York-Buffalo
Department of Biostatistics
3435 Main Street, 249 Farber Hall, Building 26
Buffalo, NY 14214-3005
716/829-2884
rcarter@buffalo.edu http://www.provost.buffalo.edu/grad/
academics/academicprograms.asp?id=210
Degrees available: Master's degree, doctorate degree

Northeastern University
Department of Biology
134 Mugar
Boston, MA 02115
617/373-2262
gradbio@neu.edu
http://www.bioinformatics.neu.edu/index.html
Degrees available: Master's degree

Ramapo College of New Jersey
Bioinformatics Program
505 Ramapo Valley Road
Mahwah, NJ 07430
201/684-7500
http://bioinformatics.ramapo.edu
Degrees available: Bachelor's degree

University of the Sciences
600 South 43rd Street
Philadelphia, PA 19104-4495
215/596-8800
http://www.usip.edu/bioinformatics
Degrees available: Bachelor's degree, master's degree

University of South Florida
College of Medicine, MDC Box 7
Department of Biochemistry and Molecular Biology
12901 Bruce B. Downs Boulevard
Tampa, FL 33612-4799
813/974-5360
bioinformatics@hsc.usf.edu
http://hsc.usf.edu/medicine/biochemistry/msbioinfocompbiol.html
Degrees available: Master's degree

University of Texas-El Paso
Bioinformatics Program Office
Bell Hall, Room 138
El Paso, TX 79968-0514
915/747-5761
bioinformatics@utep.edu
http://www.bioinformatics.utep.edu
Degrees available: Master's degree

For More Information:

American Association for the Advancement of Science
1200 New York Avenue, NW
Washington, DC 20005
http://www.aaas.org

Biotechnology Industry Organization
1225 Eye Street, NW, Suite 400
Washington, DC 20005
info@bio.org
http://www.bio.org

Interview:

Ramapo College was one of the first primarily undergraduate programs in the United States to offer a baccalaureate degree in bioinformatics. The editors of *They Teach That in College!?* spoke to Paramjeet S. Bagga, Ph.D., Associate Professor of Biology and Convener of Bioinformatics; Eric Karlin, Ph.D., (Former Dean, School of Theoretical and Applied Science); and Amruth Kumar, Ph.D., Professor of Computer Science, about Ramapo College's Bioinformatics program.

Q. Please briefly describe the bioinformatics program at Ramapo.

A. The curriculum for this program has been designed to lay a solid foundation in modern life sciences as well as cutting-edge computing technology. In advanced courses, students are trained to manage biological data, develop computational methods for analysis and integration of the data, solve scientific problems and make new discoveries. In addition to the scientific and technical concepts, students are also exposed to the social, business, and ethical dimensions of science.

Highly qualified and experienced educators teach the courses in the bioinformatics curriculum. Faculty members are actively engaged in research and often involve undergraduate students in their projects. The areas of faculty research interest include molecular biology, genomics, proteomics, structural bioinformatics, algorithms, objected-oriented programming, pharmaceutical chemistry, artificial intelligence, genetics, molecular sytematics, and database design. Bioinformatics majors may work through the cooperative education program for industrial work experience. Several of our students have presented their research accomplishments at national and international conferences, and have won many awards.

Q. How many students are involved in your program annually?

A. This is a new program. The first active recruitment for enrollment in the program began in fall 2003. At the present time there are about 25 students in the program.

Q. What types of students enter your program? What are their career goals and interests?

A. Students who have shown interest in this program have a wide variety of interests. Some students want a bachelor's degree that will enable them to find employment in the pharmaceutical, biotech, or bioinformatics industry. Many of the students plan to continue their academic efforts at the graduate level. Students who are interested in health-related professions also find our bioinformatics program very useful. In fact, we have several pre-med students in our program.

Q. What is the typical career path for a graduate of your program?

A. The Ramapo College Bioinformatics program has been very carefully designed to train students for a wide variety of career paths. The curriculum prepares students to obtain employment in the industry and academia, pursue graduate education, enter careers in medicine and related disciplines, or engage in research in this rapidly expanding technological field. Some examples of the job options for bioinformatics graduates include: research scientist, bioinformatics programmer, physician, project manager, database developer and administrator, technical assistant, and technical sales representative (some of these may require graduate education). In addition to pharmaceutical companies, potential employers include research labs in academia, hospitals, governmental agencies, software industry, and the bioinformatics service industry.

Northern New Jersey is a hub for the pharmaceutical industry and one of the largest centers for biotechnology. It houses many major companies that have high-priority programs in bioinformatics and seek individuals trained in this cutting-edge technology. Ramapo College is conveniently located near such potential employers. We have already built relationships with some of the industries to provide internship opportunities for our bioinformatics students. There are also many institutions of higher education in the area that offer graduate degrees and research opportunities in bioinformatics and related disciplines. Last year (2004), two of our graduating students were admitted into the "Genomics and

35

Computational Biology" Ph.D. program at the University of Pennsylvania.

Q. What personal qualities should a student have to be successful in your program?

A. A successful student of our bioinformatics program will have a high level of motivation to obtain technical training, aptitude for solving biological problems, and strong interests in computational science, mathematics, chemistry/biochemistry, and physics, in addition to molecular biology. By the end of undergraduate study, the student should be ready to apply the technical skills obtained and jump into ongoing research and development at the forefront of this rapidly growing field.

Q. What is the future for the program and bioinformatics in general? Do you plan to offer advanced degrees anytime soon?

A. Bioinformatics is predicted to be the next revolution in the workplace after information technology. There has been an unprecedented demand for bioinformaticians to join the forefront of research areas in industry as well as academic institutions within the last couple of years. In fact, bioinformatics is becoming one of the most sought-after skill sets in the current market.

Ramapo College of New Jersey has emerged as a role model for undergraduate education in bioinformatics. Other educational institutions are trying to follow with similar undergraduate programs. This is a much-needed effort.

Although there are some graduate-level bioinformatics programs in the United States, the number of such opportunities is insufficient to fulfill the present and future need for trained individuals. Besides, it is difficult to find suitable candidates for graduate programs. Prospective graduate students either have a biology background or have computer science background, but not both. Therefore, they have to take several additional courses to qualify for admission to graduate bioinformatics programs. If we are to address the explosive needs of the bioinformatics field, bioinformatics curriculum must be offered in institutions that are primarily undergraduate, institutions that form the bulk of schools in our country. Without programs in such undergraduate institutions, it is unlikely that we will meet the current or future needs of the bioinformatics market, and it will remain an elite discipline with a perennial shortage of a skilled workforce. Availability of undergraduate-level instruction in bioinformatics would not only start building up a highly desirable trained workforce, it would also improve the quality of graduate-level degree programs.

We also believe that the basic tools of bioinformatics will soon be widely utilized in many different fields of science. So efforts are being undertaken to incorporate the concepts and technology of bioinformatics across the entire spectrum of science courses at Ramapo College. This will ensure that all of our science students, as well as our faculty, are exposed to and understand the basic concepts of this exciting new dimension of scientific research.

We see the Ramapo College Bioinformatics program flourishing in the future. We believe that we will continue to maintain our lead role in this area. At the moment there are no plans to add a master's degree; however, we are working on establishing partnerships with institutions that already offer graduate-level study in this field.

Biomedical Photography

Students who are interested in the biological sciences and photography may want to learn more about careers in biomedical photography. Students in biomedical photography programs explore the field by learning more about digital and traditional photography and their uses in science, medicine, technology, and industry. Classroom topics include black and white and color photography, close-up and high-magnification photography, lighting, ophthalmic photography, imaging technologies, desktop publishing software, computer graphics, techniques for biomedical news and public relations photography, equipment and techniques for magnified images, and planning, executing and presenting a professional portfolio. Some colleges, such as the Ohio Institute of Photography & Technology, offer specialized areas of concentration such as photography of the patient for medical documentation, public relations, standardization of lighting in the studio, close-up photography, photomicrography, digital imaging, and video and audio-visual presentation. The Rochester Institute of Technology offers the only bachelor's degree in the field.

38

Typical Courses:

> Black and White Photography
> Color Photography
> Biomedical Photography
> Photography and the Microscope
> Digital Media
> Biology
> Desktop Publishing
> Creating a Portfolio

Potential Employers:

> Hospitals
> Colleges and universities
> Medical publishers
> Medical examiners' offices
> Forensic laboratories
> Pharmaceutical companies
> Health care and medical research centers
> Ophthalmic practices
> Producers of multimedia and web publishing

Available At:

Ohio Institute of Photography & Technology
2029 Edgefield Road
Dayton, OH 45439
800/932-9698
http://www.oipt.com/biomedical_photography.html
Degrees available: Associate degree

Randolph Community College
629 Industrial Park Avenue, PO Box 1009
Asheboro, NC 27204-1009
336/633-0200
http://www.randolph.cc.nc.us/edprog/curr/bioph.html
Degrees available: Associate degree

Fun Fact

Graduates of the Rochester Institute of Technology's biomedical photographic communications program enjoy an 85 percent job placement rate.

Rochester Institute of Technology
Department of Biomedical Photographic Communications
70 Lomb Memorial Drive
Rochester, NY 14623
biomed@rit.edu
http://biomed.rit.edu
Degrees available: Bachelor's degree

For More Information:

BioCommunications Association, Inc.
220 Southwind Lane
Hillsborough, NC 27278
919/245-0906
http://www.bca.org

Health and Science Communications Association
39 Wedgewood Drive, Suite A
Jewett City, CT 06351
860/376-5915
http://www.hesca.org

Interview: Michael Peres

The Rochester Institute of Technology (RIT) is the only school in the United States that grants a Bachelor of Science in this exciting field. The editors of *They Teach That in College!?* discussed the field of biomedical photography with Professor Michael Peres, Chair of RIT's Biomedical Photographic Communications Department.

Q. What is biomedical photography?

A. Biomedical photography might be defined as photography applied to the biological sciences. The biological sciences might include human and veterinary medicine with sub-specialties in ophthalmology and forensic science (medical examiner's office), as well as bio-research (e.g., agriculture, entomology, pharmaceuticals, etc.). In these various applications/industries, the images that are created represent data and/or scientific facts. One might characterize this type of photography as information imaging. It can include both still- and motion/time-based photography, as well as other computer imaging.

Q. Can you provide some examples of the types of biomedical subjects that are frequently photographed?

A. People who are having plastic surgery, including their pre- and post-operative conditions, might be representative of subjects of this type of photography. In dermatology, there is pre-screening photography for skin cancer where changes in moles are monitored photographically to monitor changes in color and/or size. In ophthalmic photography, retinal images are made in large numbers in a test called a fluorescein angiogram. In laboratory work, using a microscope is also common for subjects smaller than a rice grain. Depending on the application/industry, anything might be a subject.

Q. Please describe a typical student in your program.

A. The typical student is both creative and technical. He or she loves to solve problems that require the use of tools (cameras/lights) and processes that are both analytical and conceptual. An example of this might be how to develop and use a system to photograph a round transparent subject such as a contact lens, or how to create a solution to photograph something invisible such as a headache.

He or she is also self directed, like science, love photography and pictures, have analytical minds, and like using the computer to enhance and to distribute the work either through the web, through print, or with multi-media. He or she also enjoys working with people and is interested in a career in the photographic services industry.

Q. What type of co-ops or internships are available to students in your program?

A. All students are required to complete at least one co-op. The minimum co-op requirement suggests an eight-week duration that is paid and a minimum of 20 hours per week. Almost all students find a 10-week block that is full-time. We often will have approximately 15 students on co-op during a typical summer. Over the course of the last few years, some traditional sponsors include the Veterans Administration medical centers across the country, various research labs in the Smithsonian Institute, Columbia University Hospital, The Mayo Clinic, Cleveland Clinic, Zeiss Micro-Imaging, FujiFilm, and Johns Hopkins Hospital, to name a few.

Q. What types of career options are available to graduates of your program?

A. After they graduate, students are fairly open minded to many options in the job market. Ophthalmic photography continues to be the dominant career option for biomed students. There is often one job opportunity per week anywhere in the United States—with a starting salary of approximately $36,000.

Other positions exist in the pharmaceutical industry, in human medicine, in crime labs, in and veterinary schools; some graduates work as visual imaging specialists for the military or industrial sectors. Job titles include ophthalmic photographer, visual imaging expert, medical photographer, graphics specialist, technical services representative, photographic researcher, and multimedia specialist.

Q. What is the future for your program and biomedical photography in general?

A. The future for our program seems stable. Biomed is a small department, so finding employment for 12-15 highly motivated, smart imaging experts seems more than achievable. Last May, 22 students graduated—our largest class ever—and 14 students were employed at graduation. For now, the department is fixed in its capacity to take and place more students.

Biomedical photography in the United States has undergone huge changes as a consequence of significant changes in the health care industry and reimbursement procedures, as well as the complete integration of digital photography into that same industry. Ophthalmic photography is experiencing growth for now, and although this trend may slow in the next five years or so, the industry is readily accepting highly skilled people. We have also observed easy placement of our graduates into the "instructional media industry," such as companies that produce home school educational products.

Biometric Systems

Fingerprinting has been used for more than a century to identify people, primarily in the field of law enforcement, since it was determined that every human being has a unique set of fingerprints. But did you also know that our eyes, voices, and even our faces all contain unique, one-of-a-kind signatures that can be electronically measured and used for identification purposes? Today, manual fingerprinting is replaced by digital imaging, and a whole new field of study is being devoted to the development of technologies to identify humans by unique physical characteristics, no longer just for the purpose of law enforcement. Today such technology is used to restrict access in buildings where security is top priority, but it is also increasingly be used for other purposes. Banking centers are beginning to use biometric systems hoping to make pin numbers a thing of the past and decrease identity theft. Businesses use this technology as a means to clock in employees or check in members. The potential uses and applications of this technology continue to grow. The bachelor's program in biometric systems at West Virginia University is currently the only program in the country dedicated to the study of this fascinating discipline.

Typical Courses:

> Biology
> Chemistry
> Physics
> Calculus
> Microprocessor Systems
> Computer Security
> Bioengineering
> Economics
> Forensic Statistics
> Electrical Circuits
> Biometric Systems

Potential Employers:

> Law enforcement agencies
> Scientific laboratories
> Government agencies
> Private companies that build biometric systems or that integrate biometric systems into their existing products

Available At:

West Virginia University
Lane Department of Computer Science and Electrical Engineering
731 Engineering Sciences Building, PO Box 6109
Morgantown, WV 26506
304/293-LANE, ext. 2526
http://www.wvu.edu/~forensic
Degrees available: Bachelor's degree, graduate certificate

For More Information:

The Biometric Consortium
http://www.biometrics.org

Biometrics Catalog
http://www.biometricscatalog.org

Fun Fact

Biometric systems are already being used to help identify people in airports, ATMs, and in financial transactions.

Interview: Lawrence Hornak

Dr. Lawrence Hornak is a professor and biometrics advisor in the Lane Department of Computer Science and Electrical Engineering at West Virginia University (WVU), which is located in Morgantown, West Virginia. He discussed his program and the education of biometrics students with the editors of *They Teach That in College!?*

Q. What is biometrics?

A. Biometrics is a convergence of many disciplines, which is part of its attraction to students and faculty alike. Basically, a biometric system is a set of hardware and software that is optimized to capture information about a person, process it, reduce it to its bare essentials, and then compare it to previously enrolled information to see if there is a match. It is through this process that a person's identity is either ascertained or is verified. This is what biometrics is all about. Currently, the information available comes from sensors, which are basically cameras or use other data capture systems that capture aspects of the person's physiology (iris pattern, fingerprint, face, hand, voice). Eventually, one can envision this moving to a molecular realm as devices advance for this purpose.

Q. Please provide an overview of your biometrics program.

A. The biometric systems program at WVU is the only BS program in existence specifically focused on this very important area. The required curriculum of the bachelor of science degree in biometric systems is 130 credit hours.

Biometric identification is a highly interdisciplinary field. Designers work with the physics of the sensor to obtain measurements of the biometric defined by human physiology. Signal and image processing techniques are applied to the sensor signal and pattern recognition employed to extract features usable for identification. Databases combined with artificial intelligence enable rapid storage, retrieval, and pattern matching, while decision theory supports the mechanisms whereby systems can provide the needed identification results. Underlying the entire system is a foundation of statistics and mathematics that provides the language for implementing and evaluating biometric technology and systems. Given the interdisciplinary nature of the field, the program provides students with a firm foundation in electrical and computer engineering and computer science meshed with an understanding of biology, physiology, forensics, and the interaction between living and nonliving materials and systems necessary to design, implement, and evaluate biometric systems. This foundation is built on a strong framework of mathematics, statistics, and physical sciences complemented by an appropriate general studies component including psychology and physiology to give students an understanding of the human factors involved in acceptance and use of biometric systems.

Emphasis areas established through choice of specific course sets in the junior and senior year enable students to tailor their degree to follow their interests in key areas of biometric system development. Currently designated areas of

45

emphasis are Sensors and Circuits, Signal Processing, Statistics, and Software Systems.

Engineering design experiences are a central part of many of the curriculum's courses beginning in the very first semester of the program. The design experience concludes with a capstone two-semester design course in the senior year in which students form teams to plan and build biometric systems and subsystems of their own design.

Q. What are the most important qualities for biometrics majors?

A. The most successful students have a great drive to not only explore but, once they start down a path, to complete a job they have started. During the program, students who develop a mix of strong technical and interpersonal skills are the most successful. Students think engineers and systems designers work in solitary. This could not be further from the truth. In fact, most of the time they spend is in managing and working with others to effectively achieve a goal.

Q. What advice would you offer biometrics majors as they graduate and look for jobs?

A. Keep the big picture and know that there is tremendous opportunity for you to shape the future, given the fact that biometrics technology can have application in virtually all areas of day-to-day living to enable convenience, privacy, and security. Moreover, always keep in mind that especially in the area of biometrics, your greatest technical solution is only as good as people's willingness to accept it. So work on building acceptance in parallel with building the system.

Q. How is the field of biometrics changing the world in which we live?

A. As for the impact of biometrics, it is significant. Irrespective of the technological era, trust and privacy are the cornerstones of a free and democratic society. Long term, the pervasiveness achieved by information technology within our society will be enabled or inhibited by the degree to which socie-

ty perceives that it secures and strengthens these cornerstones. Whether the supporting technology be parchment or
quantum electronics, the underlying process to be upheld
remains the same. Whether the individual is boarding a
plane, purchasing online, or accessing medical records, the
efficacy of the supporting technology will be judged by its
ability to promote and preserve trust among parties through
its transparency, preservation of privacy, and resistance to
attack. To date, information technology has demonstrated a
tremendous potential to provide the framework for such
trusted processes on a global scale while at the same time
opening new opportunities for freedom of access to information, services, and products. However, realizing this potential
in an environment of rising security requirements hinges crit-
ically upon achieving robust authentication of individual
users. Biometric authentication moves beyond faceless logins
and passwords to authentication that tightly binds user
actions to the individual physical identity of the user. This is
not a short-term need precipitated by current world events
but a long-term direction prerequisite to the needed estab-
lishment of trust and preservation of privacy early in the evo-
lution of Information Technology. As embedded computing
and wireless technology extends processing power and network connectivity to virtually every object and space with
which we interact, transparent, automated human biometric
identification will be enable to achieve the trusted processes
essential for the acceptance by society of this truly pervasive
and ubiquitous computing environment.

Biotechnology

The Biotechnology Industry Organization defines biotechnology as the use of cellular and molecular processes to solve problems or make products, such as vaccines, diagnostic tests, disease-resistant crops, and so forth. Since the anthrax attacks of 2001, which made the general public aware of the threat of bioterrorism, the biotech field has gained attention. Biotech workers, after all, are the ones who work on developing ways of detecting the presence of infectious diseases as well as developing the antidotes to save us. Of course, not every biotech worker walks around in a contamination suit passing out vaccines. Areas of the industry include research and development, clinical research, manufacturing, and quality control. Since many specialties exist in biotechnology, there are many ways to train for the field. For example, scientists working in research and development may have a Ph.D. in a science field, an M.D., or both. Others who work in research and development may include laboratory assistants, research assistants, and plant breeders. These workers do not need advanced degrees such as a Ph.D. In fact, many may have diplomas or associate degrees in biotechnology. Workers in clinical research, also known as testing or validation, usually have science degrees or nursing degrees. Those in administrative positions may have more advanced degrees. Engineers in manufacturing and quality control need at least a bachelor's degree in their specialty; technicians need associate degrees. The biotechnology industry in the United States has grown rapidly, nearly quadrupling in revenues from 1992 to 2003, according to the Biotechnology Industry Organization.

48

Fun Fact

To prepare for a career in biotechnology, take as many health, biology, anatomy and physiology, mathematics, biology, chemistry, physics, English, and speech classes in high school as you can. You can also read books and visit websites about biotechnology or talk with your counselor or teacher about setting up a presentation by a biotechnology worker.

Typical Courses:

> General Biology
> General Biology Laboratory
> Cell Biology
> Molecular Biology
> Immunology
> Microbiology
> High Performance Computing for Bioinformatics
> Ethical Issues in Medicine and Biology
> Genetic Engineering
> Genomics
> Bioinformatics

Potential Employers:

> Biotechnology companies
> Agriculture industry
> Food industry
> Pharmaceutical industry
> Government agencies
> Health care industry

Available At:

The following list of biotechnolgy programs is not exhaustive. For a list of graduate programs in biotechnology, visit http://www.gradschools.com.

Camden County College
200 North Broadway
Camden, NJ 08102-1185
http://www.camdencc.edu/departments/chemistry/biotech.htm
Degrees available: Associate degree

Columbia University
Department of Biological Sciences
600 Fairchild Center, Mail Code 2402
1212 Amsterdam Avenue
New York, NY 10027
212/854-4581
biology@columbia.edu
http://www.columbia.edu/cu/biology/pages/ma-biotech/pro/intro/index.html
Degrees available: Master's degree

East Stroudsburg University of Pennsylvania
Biotechnology and Medical Technology Program
200 Prospect Street
East Stroudsburg, PA 18301-2999
570/422-3704
http://www.esu.edu/biotech/index.html
Degrees available: Bachelor's degree

Houston Community College (multiple campuses)
http://www.hccs.edu/discipline/Bitc/bitc.htmL
Degrees available: Certificate, associate degree

Iowa State University
Office of Biotechnology
1210 Molecular Biology Building
Ames, IA 50011-3260
515/294-9818
biotech@iastate.edu
http://www.biotech.iastate.edu/publications/ed_resources/
biotech_majors.html
Degrees available: Bachelor's degree

Niagara University
Biology Department
DePaul Hall of Science
Niagara University, NY 14109
800/778-3450
http://www.niagara.edu/biology
Degrees available: Bachelor's degree

Rochester Institute of Technology
58 Lomb Memorial Drive
Rochester, NY 14623
http://www.rit.edu/~932www/ugrad_bulletin/colleges/cos/
biotech.html
Degrees available: Bachelor's degree

For More Information:

Biotechnology Industry Organization
1225 Eye Street, NW, Suite 400
Washington, DC 20005
202/962-9200
info@bio.org
http://www.bio.org

Fun Fact

In 2003, approximately 198,300 people were employed in the U.S. biotechnology industry, according to the Biotechnology Industry.

National Center for Biotechnology Information
National Library of Medicine
Building 38A
Bethesda, MD 20894
301/496-2475
info@ncbi.nlm.nih.gov
http://www.ncbi.nlm.nih.gov

BioWorld Online
http://www.bioworld.com

Bowling Industry Management

Training in all phases of bowling center operations—from sales and marketing to pinsetter maintenance—makes a degree in bowling industry management a unique investment. In today's exceedingly competitive recreational industry, such highly specialized training programs position the future bowling industry manager ahead of the crowd. Vincennes University is the only college in the United States to offer a degree in bowling industry management.

Typical Courses:

> Accounting
> Lane and Pinsetter Maintenance
> Algebra
> Marketing
> Computer Science
> Business English
> Pro Shop Operations
> Personal Fitness Management
> Psychology
> Management

Potential Employers:

> Self-employment (opening your own bowling center)
> Company-owed recreational facilities
> Equipment manufacturers

Available At:

Vincennes University
College of Business and Public Service
1002 North First Street
Vincennes, IN 47591
812/888-4428
http://www.vinu.edu
Degrees available: Associate degree

Did You Know?

The International Bowling Museum and Hall of Fame, which opened in 1984, is located in St. Louis, Missouri.

For More Information:

Professional Bowlers Association
719 Second Avenue, Suite 701
Seattle, WA 98104
http://www.pba.com

Bowl.com
http://www.bowl.com

Broadcast Meteorology

F5 tornadoes, hurricanes, floods, scorching heat, blizzards. Weather plays a significant role in how we live our daily lives. And the reporting of weather conditions has become a major part of television and radio newscasts. There is even an entire television channel—The Weather Channel—devoted to keeping people informed about weather conditions around our country and the world. As a result, college programs have sprung up to train interested students in broadcast meteorology. Students should be prepared for a solid core of classes in both meteorological science and communication. While some programs offer or require a larger set of classes with a focus on media and broadcasting, all programs require a strong aptitude in the science of meteorology. Only a handful (see the list below) of colleges and universities in the United States offer degrees in broadcast meteorology.

Typical Courses:

> Science Journalism
> Algebra
> Calculus
> Physics
> News Writing
> Atmospheric Structure
> Global Physical Climatology
> Commercial Meteorology
> Speech Composition and Presentation
> Weather Analysis and Forecasting
> Television Production

Potential Employers:

> Affiliate television stations
> Cable television stations
> Public and private forecasting firms
> Environmental consulting firms
> National Weather Service
> Airlines

Available At:

Mississippi State University
Department of Geosciences
109 Hilbun Hall, PO Box 5448
Mississippi State, MS 39762-5448
662/325-3915
http://www.msstate.edu/dept/geosciences/
broadcast-meteorology.htm
Degrees available: Bachelor's degree, master's degree

State University of New York-Albany
Department of Earth and Atmospheric Sciences-ES351
Albany, NY 12222
518/442-4466
http://www.atmos.albany.edu/deas/atmbmetba.html
Degrees available: Bachelor's degree

Pennsylvania State University
Department of Meteorology
Weather Forecasting and Communications Option
503 Walker Building
University Park, PA 16802-5013
814/863-1842
meteodept@ems.psu.edu
http://www.met.psu.edu/dept/undprog
Degrees available: Bachelor's degree, master's degree, doctorate
degree

Valparaiso University
Department of Geography and Meteorology
Valparaiso, IN 46383-6493
219/464-5000
http://www.valpo.edu/geomet/met/met.html
Degrees available: Bachelor's degree

55

Fun Fact

Meteorology is one of the oldest of modern sciences. The word itself was coined by Aristotle more than 2,000 years ago for the first textbook on the science of "things lifted up."

For More Information:

American Meteorological Society
45 Beacon Street
Boston, MA 02108-3693
http://www.ametsoc.org

Broadcast Education Association
1771 N Street, NW
Washington, DC 20036-2891
http://www.beaweb.org

National Association of Broadcasters
1771 N Street, NW
Washington, DC 20036
http://www.nab.org

National Weather Association
1697 Capri Way
Charlottesville, VA 22911-3534
http://www.nwas.org

National Weather Service
1325 East-West Highway
Silver Spring, MD 20910
http://www.nws.noaa.gov

Interview: Paul Knight

Paul Knight is the director of the Weather Forecasting and Communications Option in the Department of Meteorology at Pennsylvania State University in University Park, Pennsylvania. He discussed his program and the education of broadcast meteorology students with the editors of *They Teach That in College!?*

Q. Please provide an overview of your program.

A. The Weather Communication option for a bachelor of science degree in meteorology from Penn State allows students in their last two years of undergraduate study to specialize in courses related to the communications of weather information. Students in this option, which is indicated on their diploma, are required to take approximately 20 credits of both core and elective courses in this field. The core courses include Weather Prediction, Mesoscale Meteorology, Weather Communications Part 1 And 2, and an intensive writing course.

Q. What high school subjects/activities should students focus on to be successful in this major?

A. High school students interested in pursuing a career in weather communications would be well advised to take both physics and calculus. Any options for advanced earth science courses would be recommended as well as experience in communications (school newspaper, radio, or television). Performing in theater and musical talent would also help prepare for this major.

Q. What are the most important personal and professional qualities for broadcast meteorology majors?

A. The ability to speak in front of varying size groups of people is required. It is even better if you enjoy it! A good sense of humor is necessary since everyone's forecasts go awry, and dealing with criticism in a healthy and constructive way is very important. Gaining confidence in your abilities to make a highly visible presentation as well as being willing to improve one's personal appearance are useful qualities. Ultimately, the most important is a passion for learning, especially the science of the atmosphere.

Q. How will the field of broadcast meteorology change in the future?

A. As broadcasting becomes narrow-casting due to the convergence of the Internet and television as well as the advent of hi-definition television, the opportunities for communicating weather information will increase. Computer skills related to web interface development and database management will become an important need in this field.

College of the Atlantic

The goal of the College of the Atlantic in Bar Harbor, Maine, is to help students understand and explore the relationships between humans and their environments. It offers a bachelor's and master's degree in only one field—Human Ecology—via an interdisciplinary approach to the arts and sciences. According to the College, graduates pursue careers in a variety of fields, including education, the natural sciences, art/design, social service/government, business, medical/health services, communication, and engineering. The College has intercollegiate club teams in men's and women's soccer and club squads in volleyball, basketball, and indoor soccer. It also has four clubs: the Outing Club (which organizes outdoor trips that range from day hikes to extended canoe trips), Social Environmental Action (which focuses on environmental and social issues), the Dive Club (a diving club for students), and World Citizens for Social, Environmental, and Economic Justice (an organization of students, staff, and faculty that focuses on economic, environmental, and social justice). Approximately 80 percent of students at the College of the Atlantic receive some form of financial aid.

Available Fields of Study:

Students who pursue a bachelor of arts in human ecology take classes in one of the following resource areas:
> Arts and Design
> Educational Studies
> Environmental Sciences
> Human Studies

They then develop individualized programs in one or more of the following subject areas:
> Community Development
> Environmental Science
> Humanities
> International Studies
> Landscape and Building Design
> Marine Studies
> Museum Studies
> Public Policy and Law

> Regional Studies
> Sustainable Agriculture
> Teacher Certification
> Visual and Performing Arts
> Writing, Literature

Fun Fact

The College of the Atlantic is within walking distance of Acadia National Park.

Independent work and internships are a key part of the curricula at the College. In addition, students must complete a final project (usually in the term before graduation). Recent projects included the publication of scientific research, writing a novel, recording an album of original music, creating a nonprofit educational organization, reconstructing a 4,000-square-foot seaside garden, recording the oral history of a group of former Guatemalan refugees who had been forced to resettle as a result of the Guatemalan civil war, and creating a sustainable agriculture project at a local high school.

59

Students who pursue a Master of Philosophy in Human Ecology choose nine courses that prepare them for advanced independent work in an interdisciplinary field (such as art and science) of their choice. Students complete the program by spending at least one year writing a thesis about their study area. Past thesis topics included Alternative Education, Environmental Art, Environmental History, Environmental Journalism, Environmental Literature, Graphic Arts, International Development, Land Planning, Marine Mammal Policy, Ornithology, and Technology and Society.

For More Information:

College of the Atlantic
105 Eden Street
Bar Harbor, ME 04609
inquiry@ecology.coa.edu
207/288-5015
http://www.coa.edu/html/home.htm
Degrees available: Bachelor's degree, master's degree

Computer and Digital Forensics

A new field of study is emerging from two hot career areas—computers and forensics. Computer and digital forensics combines computer know-how with the meticulous methods of forensic science. Due to the prevalence of computers in society today, many criminal activities utilize computers—creating a need for the *computer and digital forensic specialist*. Computer and digital forensic specialists work to find evidence of such things as the tampering, destruction, or copying of files, email, or instant messages. They also track such things as Internet usage and the use of restricted programs or databases. In many cases they must be careful to extract the sought-after computer data without destroying the original version, and to preserve the data in question in such a way that it will hold up in a court of law.

60

Typical Courses:

> Analysis of Digital Media
> Investigative Interviewing
> Computer Forensics
> Criminal Investigation
> Introduction to Statistics
> Computer and Network Security
> Financial Accounting
> Forensic Accounting
> Criminal Law
> Preserving/Documenting Evidence

Potential Employers:

> Law enforcement agencies
> Government agencies
> U.S. military
> Corporations
> Law firms
> Accounting firms

Available At:

The following list of colleges and universities that offer programs in computer and digital forensicsa is not exhaustive. Visit the website of the American Academy of Forensic Sciences (http://www.aafs.org) for a complete list of schools that offer training in computer forensics and other forensics-related specialties. Visit the website (http://www.e-evidence.info/education.html) for additional schools with developing programs in computer forensics and/or courses and minors in computer forensics.

California State University-Fullerton
2600 Nutwood Avenue
Fullerton, CA 92834-6870
714/278-5977
http://ueestaff.fullerton.edu/Classes/Certificate/CertDetail.asp?GN=3298&GV=1&LID
Degrees available: Certificate

Champlain College
Computer and Digital Forensics Program
163 South Willard Street, West Hall, Room 12
Burlington, VT 05401
802/865-6460
http://digitalforensics.champlain.edu
Degrees available: Certificate, associate degree, bachelor's degree

Community College of Philadelphia
1700 Spring Garden Street
Philadelphia, PA 19130
215/751-8010
http://www.ccp.edu/site/academic/degrees/computer_forensics.php
Degrees available: Associate degree

George Washington University
Department of Forensic Sciences
2036 H Street, Samson Hall
Washington, DC 20052
202/994-7319
forsc@gwu.edu
http://www.gwu.edu/~mastergw/programs/crime_commerce
Degrees available: Master's degree

Iowa Lakes Community College
300 South 18th Street
Estherville, Iowa 51334
712/362-7952
http://www.iowalakes.edu/programs_study/social_human/criminal_justice/computer_forensics.htm
Degrees available: Associate degree

Johns Hopkins University
School of Professional Studies in Business and Education
6740 Alexander Bell Drive
Columbia, MD 21046
410/312-2880
ugspsbe@jhu.edu
http://undergraduate.jhu.edu/it/
index.cfm?action=concentration&majorcode=306C&groupid=268
Degrees available: Bachelor's degree

Lake Washington Technical College
Computer Forensics and Security Program
11605 132nd Avenue, NE
Kirkland, WA 98034-8506
425/739-8100
http://lwtchost.ctc.edu/programs2/CSNT/cfor
Degrees available: Certificate, associate degree

North Carolina Wesleyan College
3400 North Wesleyan Boulevard
Rocky Mount, NC 27804-9906
877/629-2237
http://annex.ncwc.edu/adult%5Fdegree/certificate/certificate.htm
Degrees available: Certificate

Southern Utah University
Department of Computer Science
351 West University Boulevard
Cedar City, UT 8472
http://www.suu.edu/ciet/csis/cs-fs-bachelor.html
Degrees available: Bachelor's degree

Utica College
1600 Burrstone Road
Utica, NY 13502
866/295-3106
http://www.economiccrimedegrees.com
Degrees available: Certificate, bachelor's degree, master's degree

For More Information:

American Academy of Forensic Sciences
PO Box 669
Colorado Springs, CO 80901-0669
719/636-1100
http://www.aafs.org

IEEE Computer Society
1730 Massachusetts Avenue, NW
Washington, DC 20036
202/371-0101
http://www.computer.org

National Association of Forensic Accountants
2455 East Sunrise Boulevard, Suite 1201
Fort Lauderdale, FL 33304
800/523-3680
info@claimssupport.com
http://www.nafanet.com

National Center for Forensic Science
University of Central Florida
PO Box 162367
Orlando, FL 32816-2367
407/823-6469
natlctr@mail.ucf.edu
http://ncfs.ucf.edu/home.html

Interview: Gary Kessler

The Computer and Digital Forensics program at Champlain
College in Burlington, Vermont, offers certificates and associate
and bachelor's degrees in the discipline. The editors of *They
Teach That in College!?* spoke with Gary Kessler, associate pro-
fessor and program director of the Computer and Digital
Forensics and Computer Networking Programs at Champlain
College, about this interesting field.

Q. What is computer and digital forensics?

A. "Digital forensics" is the discovery, collection, and analysis of
evidence found on computers, cell phones, PDAs, digital
cameras, and other digital devices and networks. "Computer

forensics" usually refers to the analysis of computer devices, and "network forensics" refers to the analysis and interpretations of network traffic, logs, etc.

Q. Please briefly describe your program.

A. Champlain College offered its first Computer Forensics course in Fall 2002. The Computer and Digital Forensics program started in fall 2003. Since fall 2004, all courses in the program have been available online.

Champlain College's Computer and Digital Forensics program combines aspects of criminal justice, computer technology, and cybercrime. In addition to the broad general education courses, students take courses in:

✓ Criminal Justice (Basic criminal law and investigation)

✓ Computer Technology (Computers & Telecommunications, Data Communications, Operating Systems, and Information Security)

✓ Cybercrime and Forensics (Computer Forensics I & II, Analysis of Digital Media, White Collar Crime, and Forensic Accounting)

The program has been named by the National Institute of Justice Electronic Crime Partnership Initiative as the model undergraduate curriculum for e-crime education.

Q. Where will future graduates find employment opportunities?

A. We anticipate graduates finding opportunities in a number of areas:

1) Law enforcement, either as a police officer or a civilian employee of law enforcement. This area also includes government and military. Applications here would include criminal investigations and antiterrorism intelligence gathering.

2) As part of an organization's information security team, specializing in incident response, recovery, and remediation.

3) Civilian work working for third party examiners such as those at a data recovery organization, legal defense team, or accounting firm.

Q. Does your school offer any internship opportunities?

A. Due to the newness of the program we haven't yet placed too many interns. So far, we have placed individuals with local and state police agencies in their computer forensics labs. We hope to build relationships with other lab sites around the country in the upcoming year.

Q. What personal qualities should students have to be successful in your program and in their post-college career?

A. Individuals in this field need to possess an array of skills and be educationally well-rounded. More specifically, they must:

✓ Be technically knowledgeable about computers and networks

✓ Enjoy troubleshooting and solving puzzles

✓ Be aware of the legal constraints and organizational policies that guide what they can and cannot do

✓ Be willing to constantly learn about new technologies and laws

✓ Be able to communicate in both written and oral form, and be particularly able to present technical information to non-technical audiences (e.g., judges, juries, and attorneys)

Q. What is the future of computer and digital forensics? In what new areas/industries will it be used in the future?

A. Because computers and the Internet are the fastest-growing technologies being adopted by criminals and terrorists, digital forensics is and will remain a growth industry; more and more analysts will be needed in the public and private sectors.

This is a field that is also unlikely to be outsourced, particularly in the public sector where national security issues are paramount.

Computer Game Development

In the days of Pong and Pac-Man in the 1970s and 1980s, kids could only dream of designing their own computer games. Since then, computer games have grown from a novelty to a multi-billion-dollar industry. The Interactive Digital Software Association estimates that approximately 60 percent of the U.S. population plays computer and video games, and this growing interest has created a demand for computer game developers, programmers, and other professionals. In 1994, DigiPen Institute of Technology became the first school in North America to offer a two-year degree in video game programming. Today, the Institute offers associate and bachelor's degrees. In addition to DigiPen, a growing number of colleges and universities offer courses or degrees in game design and development.

Typical Courses:

> Introduction to Game Design and Production
> High Level Programming
> Algebra and Trigonometry
> Linear Algebra and Geometry
> Calculus and Planar Analytic Geometry
> Computer Graphics
> Game Implementation Techniques
> Discrete Math and Combinatorics
> 3D Computer Animation Production
> Advanced Animation and Modeling

Potential Employers:

> Computer game companies
> Educational publishers
> Any industry that requires computer simulations

Available At:

The following list of colleges that offer degrees in computer and video game development is not exhaustive. For a complete list of schools that offer computer and video game development degrees, visit http://www.igda.org/breakingin/resource_schools.php or http://www.gamasutra.com/education.

Art Institutes International (locations nationwide)
888/624-0300
http://www.artinstitutes.edu
Degrees available: Associate degree, bachelor's degree

Fun Fact

Approximately $7.3 billion in computer and video games were purchased in the United States in 2004, according to the Entertainment Software Association. Fifty-five percent of gamers are male, according to the Entertainment Software Association.

University of Baltimore
School of Information Arts and Technologies
1420 North Charles Street
Baltimore, MD 21201-5779
410/837-5473
http://iat.ubalt.edu/sde
Degrees available: Bachelor's degree

Champlain College
163 South Willard Street
Burlington, VT 05402
800/570-5858
http://www.champlain.edu/majors/egame or http://www.champlain.edu/majors/egame-prog
Degrees available: Bachelor's degree

DePaul University
Computer Science, Telecommunications and Information Systems
243 South Wabash Avenue
Chicago, IL 60604
312/362-8381
http://www.cti.depaul.edu/programs
Degrees available: Bachelor's degree

DigiPen Institute of Technology
5001-150th Avenue, NE
Redmond, WA 98052

425/558-0299
http://www.digipen.edu/main.html
Degrees available: Associate degree, bachelor's degree, master's degree

Ferris State University
Applied Technology Center
151 Fountain Street, NE
Grand Rapids, MI 49503
800/998-3425
fsugr@ferris.edu
http://www.ferris.edu/htmls/academics/atc/bachelors.html
Degrees available: Bachelor's degree

Houston Community College Southwest
Digital Gaming and Simulation
5601 West Loop South
Houston, TX 77081
713/718-5728
http://swc2.hccs.edu/digigame
Degrees available: Certificate, associate degree

Michigan State University
Department of Telecommunication, Information Studies, and Media
188 Communication Arts Building
East Lansing, MI 48824
517/432-2634
http://dmat.msu.edu/degrees/gamespecialization.html
Degrees available: Bachelor's degree, master's degree

University of Pennsylvania
Department of Computer and Information Science
3330 Walnut Street, Levine Hall
Philadelphia, PA 19104-6389
cggt@cis.upenn.edu
http://cg.cis.upenn.edu/norm and
http://www.cis.upenn.edu/grad/cggt/cggt-overview.shtml
Degrees available: Bachelor's degree, master's degree

Rochester Institute of Technology
Department of Information Technology
Student Services
102 Lomb Memorial Drive
Rochester, NY 14623-5608
585/475-6179
ITGradCoord@it.rit.edu

http://www.it.rit.edu/prosGrad.php
Degrees available: Advanced certificate

For More Information:

Entertainment Software Association
575 7th Street, NW, Suite 300
Washington, DC 20004
esa@theesa.com
http://www.theesa.com

International Game Developers Association
870 Market Street, Suite 1181
San Francisco, CA 94102-3002
415/738-2104
info@igda.org
http://www.igda.org

Interview: Andy Phelps

The Rochester Institute of Technology (RIT) offers an Advanced Certificate in Interactive Multimedia Development and a concentration in Game Programming. It will also soon offer a Master's degree in Game Design & Development. The editors of *They Teach That in College!?* spoke with Andy Phelps, Assistant Professor in the Department of Information Technology at RIT, about his interesting program.

Q. What types of students take the concentration? What are their career goals and interests? Have you had a good response from students since the concentration was created?

A. Ninety-five percent of the students in the concentration want to get a job programming games. The others are there because they have an interest in virtual worlds and simulation. We have had excellent student response [to the program]. They are very happy with it thus far, and we are constantly seeking their feedback for improvement.

Q. What type of career path does the average student take upon graduating from your program?

A. Generally, they are instantly employed. Some are immediately employed by [electronics] game companies, and others take more corporate-oriented jobs until they find the position they think is right for them.

Q. What high school subjects/activities should students focus on to be successful in this field?

A. Were I in high school, and I wanted to get into the games and entertainment industry, what I would study would depend a lot on how I saw myself fitting into the industry. For the aspiring developer, courses in physics, mathematics, and entry-level computer science would be important. For aspiring artists, courses in painting, drawing, etc. For EVERYONE interested in getting into the gaming industry, being able to communicate is key-a focus on written English, creative writing, and spelling and grammar is critical. If you ever want to write games or create game worlds, a careful study of historical periods can be very helpful. In short, I would pay attention to everything, and constantly think about how the material can be co-opted into the study and creation of games.

Q. What personal qualities do students need to be successful in your program and in their post-college careers?

A. They should be self-driven more than anything else. If you're not pushing yourself to eat, sleep, and breathe this stuff, no one else will. There are tons of people to help you on campus and, believe it or not, there are people who will help you get into the game industry. But you really have to want it. You have to be willing to put that first. Don't expect everyone to instantly know who you are and how great you are. You have to prove it. In school, it's easier because you have faculty testing you and pushing you, as well as friends and family behind you. Once you get out in the work world, you have to do it yourself.

Q. Can you tell us about your new Masters in Game Design & Development? What type of classes are involved? When will it be available?

A. If all goes well, and New York State approves, we hope to start as early as fall of 2006. However, we are still moving through the approval process, so I can't say for sure. Our curricular design is centered around blending the backbone of computing with the development and artistic design of game production. Students take a major and minor sequence in a technical area, as well as a series of core seminars that address the breadth of the industry, including issues surrounding the bridge between technical computing and experience design. Finally, students work in teams to complete a capstone experience that includes both individual and group goals. Their final solutions are shown to industry at an annual defense/exhibition.

Conflict Resolution and Peace Studies

The 20th century and the early years of the 21st century have been marked by world wars, regional conflicts, ethnic cleansing, and terrorist attacks. Many people have sought to find nonviolent solutions to the world's problems. Conflict resolution and peace studies majors explore the exciting frontiers of nonviolent alternatives to conflict—alternatives that do not tear down, but work to build positive relations between adversaries. The core requirements of this major are drawn from different departments: political science, psychology, economics, philosophy, and religion. In the modern, globalized world, conflict intervention that fosters peace between world leaders and governments is becoming increasingly vital. Yet peacebuilding and conflict resolution initiatives and activities within local, regional, statewide, and national communities are also important. Graduates are prepared to contribute to peacebuilding in conflict and post-conflict societies as well as their own local and national communities.

Typical Courses:

> International Politics
> Religions and War
> Sociology of Violence and Non-Violence
> Analysis of War and Peace
> Conflict Analysis and Resolution
> Social Movements
> Philosophy of Religion
> Cultural Anthropology
> International Economics and Law
> Cross-Cultural Psychology

Potential Employers:

> Peace research organizations
> Social service agencies
> Citizens' action organizations
> Universities and colleges
> Humanitarian nonprofit organizations
> Government agencies, the United Nations, and related agencies

Available At:

It is estimated that one-third of our nation's 221 Roman Catholic Colleges and universities offer some type of Peace Studies program or classes. Visit the website of the Association of Catholic Colleges and Universities (http://www.accunet.org) for a searchable list of institutions.

American University
The School of International Service
4400 Massachusetts Avenue, NW
Washington, DC 20016-8071
202/885-1600
sisgrad@american.edu
http://www.american.edu/academic.depts/sis/academics/
fieldofstudy/ipcr.htm
Degrees available: Master's degree

Chapman University
Department of Political Science
1 University Drive
Orange, CA 92866
714/997-6620
http://www.chapman.edu/wcls/peacestudies
Degrees available: Bachelor's degree

73

Fun Fact

Student practicums—the opportunity to explore what a career in conflict resolution is really like—often involve international travel to countries such as Jamaica, Bosnia, Northern Ireland, Kosovo, or Indonesia, where students focus on issues such as social justice, human rights, disarmament, and world hunger.

Colgate University
Alumni Hall
Hamilton, NY 13346
315/228-7806
peace@mail.colgate.edu
http://www.colgate.edu/
DesktopDefault1.aspx?tabid=683&pgID=3210&dID=39&srtID=2
Degrees available: Bachelor's degree

University of Denver
Conflict Resolution Institute
2201 South Gaylord Street
Denver, CO 80208
303/871-6477
cri@du.edu
http://www.du.edu/con-res
Degrees available: Master's degree

Georgetown University
Department of Government
3240 Prospect Street, NW, Lower Level
Washington, DC 20057
202/687-0519
http://conflictresolution.georgetown.edu
Degrees available: Master's degree

Loyola University Chicago
Interdisciplinary Programs-Peace Studies
6430 North Kenmore Avenue, Damen Hall 914
Chicago, IL 60626
773/508-3068
http://www.luc.edu/depts/peace_st
Degrees available: Bachelor's degree

Kennesaw State University
Department of Political Science and International Affairs
1000 Chastain Road
MB 2302
Kennesaw, GA 30144-5591
770/423-6299
http://www.kennesaw.edu/pols/mscm
Degrees available: Master's degree

Manchester College
Peace Studies Institute
604 East College Avenue, PO Box 105
North Manchester, IN 46962-1276
260/982-5343
http://www.manchester.edu/academic/programs/departments/pea
ce_studies/academic.html
Degrees available: Bachelor's degree

Portland State University
Conflict Resolution Program
PO Box 751

Did You Know?

The Nobel Foundation provides the Nobel Prize to individuals and organizations that strive for peaceful resolutions to world conflict. Past recipients include Jimmy Carter, former President of the United States; Nelson Mandela, leader of the African National Congress; and Elie Wiesel, Chairman of The President's Commission on the Holocaust, author, and humanitarian. For more information, visit http://nobelprize.org/index.html.

Portland, OR 97207-0751
503-725-9175
http://www.conflictresolution.pdx.edu
Degrees available: Master's degree

Salisbury University
Department of Sociology
FH 266
Salisbury, MD 21801
410/219-2873
conflictresolution@salisbury.edu
http://www.salisbury.edu
Degrees available: Bachelor's degree

For More Information:

Center for Conflict Resolution, Inc.
1100 Camden Avenue
Salisbury, MD 21801
410/219-2873
http://www.conflict-resolution.org/sitebody/education/domestic.htm

U.S. Institute of Peace
1200 17th Street, NW
Washington, DC 20036
202/457-1700
http://www.usip.org

Construction Management

Every building, big or small, that makes up the skyline of your town or city has been constructed under the vision and management of a few key individuals—the *construction manager* among them. Construction managers work with architects, building owners, contractors, and tradesworkers to oversee the development of a variety of projects, including residential housing, commercial construction such as stores and shopping malls, skyscrapers, transportation systems, municipal services, and utilities. College degree programs in construction management typically include many industry-specific courses, combined with business courses in operations, finance, and marketing. Degrees in construction management are available at all academic levels. Opportunities for graduates of construction management programs are good. In fact, according to the U.S. Department of Labor, employment in construction is projected to increase by 15 percent from 2002 to 2012.

76

Typical Courses:

> Building the Human Environment
> Construction Methods
> Concrete and Concrete Form Systems
> Surveying and Building Layout
> Structural Steel Systems
> Construction Estimating and Bidding
> Electrical Systems
> Soil Mechanics
> Construction Safety and Risk Management
> Heavy Civil and Highway Construction
> Field Work Experience

Potential Employers:

> General contractors
> Specialty contractors such as mechanical, plumbing, and electrical
> Architectural firms
> Engineering firms
> Governmental agencies

Available At:

The following list of colleges that offer degrees in construction management is not exhaustive. For a complete listing of accredited two- and four-year programs in construction management, visit the American Council for Construction Education's website at http://www.acce-hq.org.

Alfred State College
Department of Civil Engineering Technology
10 Upper College Drive
Alfred, NY 14802
607/587-4215
http://www.alfredstate.edu/alfred/
Construction_Management_Engineering.asp?SnID=490366783
Degrees available: Bachelor's degree

Auburn University
Department of Building Science
119 Dudley Hall
Auburn, AL 36849-5315
334/844-4518
http://www.bsci.auburn.edu
Degrees available: Bachelor's degree, master's degree

Boise State University
Department of Construction Management and Engineering
1910 University Drive
Boise, ID 83725
208/426-3764
amaccarillo@boisestate.edu
http://coen.boisestate.edu/cm/home.asp
Degrees available: Bachelor's degree

Central Washington University
Department of Industrial and Engineering Technology
400 East University Way
Ellensburg, WA 98926-7584
509/963-1756
carnsd@cwu.edu
http://www.cwu.edu/~iet/programs/cmgt/cmgt.html
Degrees available: Bachelor's degree

Edmonds Community College
Construction Management Department
20000 68th Avenue West
Lynwood, WA 98036

425/640-1026
const@edcc.edu
http://const.edcc.edu
Degrees available: Certificate, associate degree

Indiana State University
Department of Manufacturing and Construction Technology
200 North Seventh Street
Terre Haute, IN 47809
812/237-3377
mct@indstate.edu
http://www.indstate.edu/mct/ct.htm
Degrees available: Bachelor's degree, master's degree, doctorate degree

John Brown University
Department of Construction Management
2000 West University Street
Siloam Springs, AR 72761
479/524-9500
http://www.jbu.edu/academics/engineering/cm/index.asp
Degrees available: Bachelor's degree

Louisiana State University
Department of Construction Management
3128 CEBA Building
Baton Rouge, LA 70803-6419
225/578-5112
cm@lsu.edu
http://www.cm.lsu.edu
Degrees available: Bachelor's degree

New York City Technical College
Construction Civil Engineering Technology
300 Jay Street, Voorhees Hall 433 (V-433)
Brooklyn, NY 11201-2983
718/260-5575
tcioffi@citytech.cuny.edu
http://www.citytech.cuny.edu/academics/deptsites/
constructiontech/index.shtml
Degrees available: Associate degree

University of North Florida
Department of Building Construction Management
4567 Saint Johns Bluff Road South
Jacksonville, FL 32224-2645

904/620-2683
http://www.unf.edu/ccec/bcm
Degrees available: Bachelor's degree, master's degree

North Lake College
Construction Management and Technology
5001 North MacArthur Boulevard
Irving, TX 75038
972/273-3000
http://www.northlakecollege.edu/academics/ConTech/conmgt.htm
Degrees available: Associate degree

Northern Arizona University
College of Engineering and Natural Sciences
Beaver Street, Building #22
Flagstaff, AZ 86011
928/523-4679
http://www.cet.nau.edu/Academic/CM
Degrees available: Bachelor's degree

State Fair Community College
Department of Applied Science and Technology
Fielding Technical Center
3201 West 16th Street
Sedalia, MO 65301-2199
660/530-5800
bloess@sfcc.cc.mo.us
http://www.sfcc.cc.mo.us/pages/206.asp
Degrees available: Associate degree

Triton College
School of Technology
2000 Fifth Avenue
River Grove, IL 60171-1995
708/456-0300
triton@triton.edu
http://www.triton.edu/cgi-bin/r.cgi/
department_detail.html?SESSION=k1vDG2eZxv&ContentID=126
Degrees available: Associate degree

For More Information:

American Council for Construction Education
1717 North Loop 1604 East, Suite 320
San Antonio, TX 78232-1570
acce@acce-hq.org
http://www.acce-hq.org

Court and Real-Time Reporting

Court reporters use stenotype machines to record legal proceedings in courtrooms. *Real-time reporters* combine shorthand machine reporting with computer-aided transcription to provide real-time testimony in courtrooms and other settings. Other professionals help people with hearing or visual disabilities by creating closed captioning for television shows, radio broadcasts, and movies, as well as in classrooms and other settings. An associate degree in court reporting is required to work in the field.

Typical Courses:

> Theory
> Introduction to Computer-Aided Transcription
> Speed Development
> Realtime Reporting Punctuation and Proofreading
> Realtime Concepts
> Introduction to Transcription Preparation
> Technical Dictation
> Principles of Captioning/CART
> Captioning/CART Speed Development
> Medical Terminology and Anatomy
> Legal Terminology

Potential Employers:

> Courts
> Law firms
> Broadcasting companies
> Organizations that provide services to the deaf

Available At:

The following list of colleges that offer degrees in court reporting is not exhaustive. Visit http://www.ncraonline.org/education/schools/index.shtml for a complete list of programs.

Academy of Court Reporting
(six campuses in Michigan, Ohio, and Pennsylvania)

80

http://www.acr.edu
Degrees available: Associate degree

Albuquerque Technical Vocational Institute
525 Buena Vista, SE
Albuquerque, NM 87106
505/224-3000
http://www.tvi.cc.nm.us
Degrees available: Associate degree

Alfred State College
215 EJ Brown Hall
Alfred, NY 14802
800/4-ALFRED
http://www.alfredstate.edu
Degrees available: Associate degree

Alvin Community College
3110 Mustang Road
Alvin, TX 77511
281/756-3500
http://www.alvincollege.edu
Degrees available: Associate degree

Cerritos College
11110 Alondra Boulevard
Norwalk, CA 90650
562/860-2451
http://www.cerritos.edu
Degrees available: Associate degree

Chattanooga State Technical College
4501 Amnicola Highway
Chattanooga, TN 37406-1097
423/697-4400
http://www.chattanoogastate.edu
Degrees available: Associate degree

Clark State Community College
570 East Leffel Lane
Springfield, OH 45505
937/325-0691
http://www.clark.cc.oh.us
Degrees available: Associate degree

Community College of Allegheny County
808 Ridge Avenue
Pittsburgh, PA 15212-2748
412/237-4600
http://www.ccac.edu
Degrees available: Associate degree

Cuyahoga Community College
700 Carnegie Avenue
Parma, OH 44115
216/987-5112
http://www.tri-c.edu/ccr/Default.htm
Degrees available: Associate degree

Gadsden State Community College
PO Box 227
Gadsden, AL 35902-0227
256/549-8200
http://www.gadsdenstate.edu
Degrees available: Associate degree

GateWay Community College
108 North 40th Street
Phoenix, AZ 85034
602/286-8000
http://business.gatewaycc.edu/Programs/
RealTimeClosedCaptioning/default.htm
Degrees available: Associate degree

Green River Community College
12401 SE 320th Street
Auburn, WA 98092
253/833-9111
http://www.greenriver.edu
Degrees available: Associate degree

Hinds Community College
PO Box 1100
Raymond, MS 39154-1100
800/HINDS-CC
Degrees available: Associate degree

Huntington Junior College
900 Fifth Avenue
Huntington, WV 25701
304/697-7550, 800/344-4522

http://www.huntingtonjuniorcollege.com/
Real-timeReporting.htm
Degrees available: Associate degree

Key College
225 East Dania Beach Boulevard
Dania, FL 33004
954/923-4440
http://www.keycollege.edu/page9.html
Degrees available: Associate degree

Las Vegas College
170 North Stephanie Street, Suite 125
Henderson, NV 89074
888/741-4270
http://lasvegas-college.com
Degrees available: Associate degree

Lenoir Community College
231 Highway 58 South, PO Box 188
Kinston, NC 28502-0188
252/527-6223
http://www.lenoir.cc.nc.us/nsite/academicprogs/crt/courtreport.html
Degrees available: Associate degree

Madison Area Technical College
3550 Anderson Street
Madison, WI 53704
608/246-6100, 800/322-6282
http://matcmadison.edu/matc/ASP/showprogram.asp?ID=3055
Degrees available: Associate degree

Metropolitan College
10820 East 45th Street, Building B, Suite 101
Tulsa, OK 74136
918/627-9429
http://www.metropolitancollege.edu/prod02.htm
Degrees available: Associate degree

Miami Dade Community College (multiple campuses)
305/237-8888
https://sisvsr.mdc.edu/ps/sheet.aspx
Degrees available: Associate degree

Midlands Technical College
PO Box 2408

Columbia, SC 29202
803/738-8324, 800/922-8038
http://www.midlandstech.edu/edu/ed/ISM/CPT/programs/crp.htm
Degrees available: Associate degree

Fun Fact

Court reporters earned an average annual salary of $62,000 in 2004, according to the National Court Reporters Association.

University of Mississippi
PO Box 1848
University, MS 38677-1848
662/915-7226
http://www.olemiss.edu
Degrees available: Associate degree

South Suburban College
Court Reporting Program
15800 South State Street
South Holland, IL 60473-1200
708/596-2000
http://www.ssc.cc.il.us/acad/career/depts/legalstudies/courtreport.htm
Degrees available: Associate degree

West Kentucky Community and Technical College
4810 Alben Barkley Drive, PO Box 7380
Paducah, KY 42002-7380
270/554-9200
http://business.westkentucky.kctcs.edu/legal
Degrees available: Associate degree

For More Information:

National Court Reporters Association
8224 Old Courthouse Road
Vienna, VA 22182-3808
800/272-6272
http://www.verbatimreporters.com

National Verbatim Reporters Association
207 Third Avenue
Hattiesburg, MS 39401
601/582-4345
http://www.nvra.org

Dance Therapy

Dance therapists, sometimes called *movement therapists,* create and conduct dance sessions to assist physically, emotionally, and mentally ill people. Dance therapists also use these sessions to help doctors and rehabilitation specialists determine an individual's progress in rehabilitation. Students become dance therapists by completing a master's degree program in dance therapy—some of which are approved by the American Dance Therapy Association (ADTA). Others receive dance therapy training to supplement a master's degree in dance or in a mental health field. Undergraduate coursework in dance therapy is also available.

Typical Classes:

> Neuroanatomy/Neurophysiology
> Anatomy and Kinesiology
> Developmental Body Movement
> Introduction to Dance/Movement
> Movement Observation
> Dance/Movement Therapy Clinical Practicum
> Family Dance/Movement Therapy
> Applied Ethics for the Creative Arts Therapies
> Theories in Psychotherapy
> Medical Dance/Movement Therapy
> The Kestenberg Movement Profile
> Laban Movement Analysis

Potential Employers:

> Adult day care centers
> After-school programs
> Hospitals
> Mental health facilities
> Nursing homes
> Private practice
> Schools
> Substance abuse treatment centers
> Community Centers
> Rehabilitation Facilities

Available At:

Antioch New England Graduate School
Department of Applied Psychology
40 Avon Street
Keene, NH 03431-3552
admissions@antiochne.edu
800/553-8920
http://apdept.antiochne.edu/ap/dmt
Degrees available: Master's degree

Columbia College Chicago
Graduate Dance/Movement Therapy Program
624 South Michigan, Room 1100
Chicago, IL 60605-1996
312/344-7697
http://www.colum.edu/graduate/04-05/graddance.html
Degrees available: Master's degree, graduate certificate

Drexel University
Center City Health Sciences Campus
Hahnemann Creative Arts in Therapy Program
245 North 15th Street, Mail Stop #905
Philadelphia, PA 19102-1192
215/762-7851
http://www.drexel.edu/cnhp/dance_movement/about.asp
Degrees available: Master's degree

Lesley University
29 Everett Street
Cambridge, MA 02138
617/349-8413
http://www.lesley.edu/faculty/estrella/dance.html
Degrees available: Master's degree

Naropa University
Dance/Movement therapy Concentration
Somatic Psychology Program
Paramita Campus
3285 30th Street
Boulder, CO 80302
800/772-6951
http://www.naropa.edu/somatic/index.html
Degrees available: Master's degree

Pratt Institute
Graduate Dance/Movement Therapy Program.
200 Willoughby Avenue, East Hall 3
Brooklyn NY 11205
718/636-3428
lthompso@pratt.edu
http://www.pratt.edu/ad/ather
Degrees available: Master's degree

For a list of alternative training opportunities, visit the ADTA's
website, http://www.adta.org/resources/education.cfm.

For More Information:

American Dance Therapy Association
2000 Century Plaza, Suite 108
10632 Little Patuxent Parkway
Columbia, MD 21044
410/997-4040
info@adta.org
http://www.adta.org

Deaf Studies

Approximately 32.5 million people in the United States are deaf or hard of hearing, according to the U.S. Census Bureau. As government, and society as a whole, has become more aware of the rights and needs of people who are deaf, exciting career opportunities have emerged for persons interested in professional work in deaf-related fields. To meet this demand, colleges are adding or improving their deaf studies programs, which teach students about deaf history, culture, and sign language. The academic discipline of deaf studies is a growing field, as increased understanding of the deaf community—within the broader national and international community—is necessary.

Typical Classes:

> Basic Sign Language
> Introduction to American Sign Language
> Sign Mime and Creative Movement
> Introduction to Deaf Studies
> Structure of American Sign Language
> Deaf Art/Deaf Artists
> Deaf Theater History
> Organizational Communication and the Deaf Employee
> Deaf Culture and Community
> Introduction to American Sign Language Teaching
> Civil Rights and Deaf People

Potential Employers:

> Human services organizations
> Government agencies
> Schools
> Deaf-related associations and organizations
> Employment agencies that serve the deaf or hard of hearing

Available At:

Boston University
Department of Literacy and Language, Counseling and Development
One Sherborn Street
Boston, MA 02215

617/353-3205 (Voice/TTY)
http://www.bu.edu/education/students/prospective/
undergraduate/programs/deaf/
Degrees available: Bachelor's degree

California State University-Northridge
Department of Deaf Studies
Education Building, Room 1107
18111 Nordhoff Street
Northridge, CA 91330
818/677-5116 (Voice), 818/677-4973 (TTY)
deaf.studies@csun.edu
http://www.csun.edu/~sch_educ/dfst/index.html
Degrees available: Bachelor's degree

Gallaudet University
Department of ASL and Deaf Studies
800 Florida Avenue, NE, Hall Memorial Building, Room E-111
Washington, DC 20002-3695
202/651-5814
http://depts.gallaudet.edu/deaf.studies/about.htm
Degrees available: Bachelor's degree, master's degree

LaGuardia Community College
Natural and Applied Sciences Department
31-10 Thomson Avenue
Long Island City, NY 11101
718/482-7200
http://www.lagcc.cuny.edu/hsp/hsp2/deaf.htm
Degrees available: Associate degree

Rochester Institute of Technology
National Technical Institute for the Deaf
52 Lomb Memorial Drive
Rochester, NY 14623
585/475-6809 (Voice/TTY), 585/475-6851 (TTY)
http://www.rit.edu/~932www/ugrad_bulletin/colleges/ntid/
specert.html#deafstudies
Degrees available: Certificate

Seattle Central Community College
Allied Health, Business, Languages, and Cultures Division
1701 Broadway, Room 2BE3210
Seattle, WA 98122
http://seattlecentral.edu/proftech/PROdeafstudies.php
Degrees available: Associate degree

Towson University
Department of Audiology, Speech-Language Pathology and Deaf
Studies
8000 York Road
Towson, MD 21252-0001
410/704-2436 (Voice/TTY)
http://wwwnew.towson.edu/asld/deaf.htm
Degrees available: Bachelor's degree

For More Information:

**Alexander Graham Bell Association
for the Deaf and Hard of Hearing**
3417 Volta Place, NW
Washington, DC 20007-2778
202/337-5220, 202/337-5221 (TTY)
info@agbell.org
http://www.agbell.org

American Speech-Language-Hearing Association
10801 Rockville Pike
Rockville, MD 20852
800/498-2071, 301/897-5700 (TTY)
actioncenter@asha.org
http://www.asha.org

Deep Springs College

A Two-Year Liberal Arts Education for Free? The catch: students at Deep Springs College—a 26-student, male-only institution with a working cattle ranch and alfalfa farm—must perform manual labor in exchange for their tuition (a $35,000 value). Duties might include milking cows, baling hay, cooking breakfast, scrubbing toilets, or mopping floors. Classes—typically one or two a day—are usually held in the morning with work done in the early morning (before classes) and in the afternoon. Deep Springs College is highly selective (the average SAT score of students is 1450) and rarely accepts more than 15 percent of applicants. It has an excellent reputation for preparing students for work and life in general; many of its graduates go on to pursue bachelor's degrees at top schools such as Harvard, Yale, Stanford, Columbia, Oxford, University of California-Berkeley, and Cornell. Deep Springs College was founded by Lucien Lucius Nunn, a mining magnate, in 1917. Its founding principles are academics, labor, and self-governance. The average class size at Deep Springs College is four!

Available Fields of Study:

Instruction is offered in the humanities, in the social sciences, and in the natural sciences and mathematics. Students are free to choose coursework from any of these areas but are required to take composition and public speaking.

For More Information:

Deep Springs College
HC72 Box 45001
Dyer, NV 89010-9803
760/872-2000
http://www.deepsprings.edu
Degrees available: Associate degree

Digital Media

Turn on your television and you will be unable to escape a barrage of advertisements for the latest cellular phone—and it probably shoots videos, sends email, and more. This is just one example of emerging digital media. Ten years ago there would have been those among us who had never used the Internet, and the idea of digital radios, televisions, or cameras was just a dream. Today, digital media is commonplace in today's modern world. As a result, colleges across the country have been developing degree programs in this emerging field. After all, someone needs to be skilled in producing the content for all forms of existing and emerging digital media! Prospective students should have a desire for a truly multidisciplinary course of study. Courses housed in the departments of art, communications, engineering, and computer science are required. If developing digital media for DVDs, CD-ROMs, and the Internet; creating video projects; and capturing and manipulating video, image, and audio files sounds fun to you, then a degree in digital media studies will be the first step into this fast-growing field.

92

Typical Courses:

> Digital Video Art
> Interactive Art and Design
> Digital Design Concepts
> Field Production and Editing
> Web Building and Site Management
> Web Application Development
> Telecommunication and Internet Law
> Technical Foundations of Digital Media
> Digital Animation
> 2D and 3D Design

Potential Employers:

> Advertising agencies
> Graphic design firms
> Film and television companies
> Game design firms
> Book and publishing companies
> Corporate art and graphic design departments

Available At:

Canisius College
Department of Communication Studies
2001 Main Street, Lyons Hall, Room 314
Buffalo, NY 14208-1098
716/888-2115
http://www.canisius.edu/comm_stud/dma
Degrees available: Bachelor's degree

University of Denver
Digital Media Studies
2000 East Asbury Street, Sturm Hall 216
Denver, CO 80208
303/871-7716
http://dms.du.edu/main/about.cfm
Degrees available: Bachelor's degree, master's degree

Gibbs College-Norwalk
10 Norden Place
Norwalk, CT 06855-1436
800/845-5333
http://www.gibbsnorwalk.edu/digital.asp
Degrees available: Associate degree

Marist College
School of Communication and the Arts
3399 North Road
Poughkeepsie, NY 12601
845/575-3000, ext. 2309
http://www.marist.edu/commarts/art/digitalmajor.html
Degrees available: Bachelor's degree

Valencia Community College
Department of Digital Media Technology
PO Box 3028
Orlando, FL 32802-3028
http://valenciacc.edu/IToptions/job_digitalmedia.asp
Degrees available: Associate degree

For More Information:

International Digital and Media Arts Association
Ball State University
CICS, BC221
Muncie, IN 47306
http://www.idmaa.org

Drama Therapy

According to the National Association for Drama Therapy (NADT), drama therapy is "the intentional use of drama and/or theater processes to achieve therapeutic goals." Therapy methods used include pantomime, role-playing, puppetry, theater games, storytelling, improvisation, and original scripted dramatization. Students become drama therapists by attending drama therapy master's or doctoral degree programs that are approved by the NADT. There are only two such programs in the United States and one in Canada. Others who have advanced degrees in theater or mental health fields prepare for the field by receiving drama therapy training via the NADT's alternative training program.

Typical Courses:

> Introduction to Drama Therapy
> Drama Therapy Process and Technique
> Drama Therapy Practice
> Creative Dramatics
> Psychodrama
> Drama Therapy with Special Populations
> Theater Lab: Advanced Improvisation and Group Process
> Special Methods in Drama Therapy
> Theories of Individual and Family Therapy

Potential Employers:

> Adult day care centers
> After-school programs
> Corporations
> Correctional facilities
> Hospitals
> Mental health facilities
> Nursing homes
> Private practice
> Schools
> Substance abuse treatment centers
> Theaters

Available At:

California Institute of Integral Studies
Drama Therapy Program
1453 Mission Street
San Francisco, CA 94103
415/575-6100
http://www.ciis.edu/academics/pdt.html
Degrees available: Master's degree

Concordia University
Department of Creative Arts Therapies
Master's Programme in Creative Arts Therapies
1455 de Maisonneuve Boulevard, West
Montreal, QB H3G 1M8 Canada
514/848-2424, ext. 4790
http://art-therapy.concordia.ca/dr_index.htm
Degrees available: Master's degree

New York University
Music and Performing Arts Professions
Drama Therapy Program
35 West 4th Street, Suite 777
New York, NY 10012-1172
212/998-5402
nyudramatherapy@yahoo.com
http://education.nyu.edu/music/drama
Degrees available: Master's degree

For a list of alternative training opportunities, visit the National Association for Drama Therapy's website, http://www.nadt.org/alttrainopptys.html.

For More Information:

National Association for Drama Therapy
15 Post Side Lane
Pittsford, NY 14534
585/381-5618
answers@nadt.org
http://www.nadt.org

Electronic Commerce

Online retailing has become big business—an essential component to every retailer's sales plan. What critics once thought would never catch on—has. Consumers around the world have gotten over their fear of giving out their personal information electronically and continue to make the Internet an ever-expanding marketplace. There is hardly anything that you CAN'T purchase online today. Purchasing items while sitting at your computer, in the comfort of your own home, is indeed a phenomenon that marketers, retailers, and business owners have to study. As a result, programs focused on this new e-commerce phenomenon have sprung up, attracting more and more students into this new field. While all programs combine core courses in business and technology, students with a particular interest in one or the other should be aware that some programs are more business-based, that is, they focus on how to attract online customers and expand online sales, while others are technological-based, focusing on the engineering fundamentals that make it possible to buy a car at the click a mouse button. Degrees in electronic commerce and related fields are available at all academic levels.

Typical Courses:

> E-Commerce Website Engineering
> Data Communications
> Object Oriented Modeling
> Technical Fundamentals of Distributed Information
> Intranets and Portals
> Internet Supply Chain Management
> Secure Electronic Commerce
> Internet Marketing
> Software Project Development and Management
> Java Programming

Potential Employers:

> Internet-based or communications-related businesses
> Traditional product/service companies using electronic commerce
> Consulting companies in the virtual or actual marketplace

Available At:

Bellevue University
Fred H. Hawkins College of Professional Studies
1000 Galvin Road South
Bellevue, NE 68005
800/756-7920
Degrees available: Bachelor's degree

Did You Know?

Amazon.com sold more than $2.27 billion worth of books, CDs, and DVDs in 2003.

Carnegie Mellon University
Graduate School of Industrial Administration
Electronic Commerce Program
GSIA 208
5000 Forbes Avenue
Pittsburgh, PA 15213
412/268-1322
http://www.mism.cmu.edu/courses/specializations/ecommerce.asp
Degrees available: Master's degree

Clarkson University
School of Business
8 Clarkson Avenue
Potsdam, NY 13699
315/268-6400
admission@clarkson.edu
http://www.clarkson.edu/programs_of_study/programs/ebusiness.html
Degrees available: Bachelor's degree

DePaul University
School of Computer Science, Telecommunications, and
Information Systems
243 South Wabash Avenue
Chicago, IL 60604
312/362-8381
cti@cti.depaul.edu
http://www.cs.depaul.edu/programs/2005/BachelorECT2005.asp
Degrees available: Bachelor's degree, master's degree

Milwaukee Area Technical College (four campuses in Wisconsin)
414/297-6282
http://mktgcamp.matc.edu/ecommerce/index.aspx
Degrees available: Associate degree

Pellissippi State Technical Community College
10915 Hardin Valley Road
Knoxville, TN 37933-0990
865/694-6400
http://www.pstcc.edu/community_relations/catalog/
ctp/programs/emarke.html
Degrees available: Associate degree

Sheridan College
Computer Web Development and Internet Business Program
3059 Coffeen Avenue
Sheridan, WY 82801
307/674-6446
http://www.sheridan.edu/programs/ecommerce.asp
Degrees available: Associate degree

For More Information:

Information Technology Association of America
1401 Wilson Boulevard, Suite 1100
Arlington, VA 22209
703/522-5055
http://www.itaa.org

Embry-Riddle Aeronautical University

If you've always had a special place in your heart for airplanes, space shuttles, and related technology, you might want to learn more about Embry-Riddle Aeronautical University, the only accredited, aviation-oriented university in the world. Embry-Riddle offers more than 30 baccalaureate- and graduate-level aviation/aerospace majors. The University has residential campuses in Daytona Beach, Florida, and Prescott, Arizona. It offers intercollegiate (baseball, basketball, cross country, golf, soccer, tennis, wrestling, and volleyball) sports, recreational and intramural sports activities, and more than 100 clubs and organizations for its students. Ninety-three percent of residential students at Embry-Riddle receive some form of financial aid.

Available Fields of Study:

Bachelor's Degree Programs
> Aeronautical Science
> Aviation Maintenance Science
> Aeronautics
> Aerospace Electronics
> Aerospace Engineering
> Aerospace Studies
> Air Traffic Management
> Applied Meteorology
> Aviation Business Administration
> Aviation Management
> Civil Engineering
> Communication
> Computer Engineering
> Computer Science
> Computer Science/Master of Software Engineering (combined five-year bachelor's and master's program)
> Electrical Engineering
> Engineering Physics
> Global Security and Intelligence Studies
> Human Factors Psychology/Human Factors and Systems (combined five-year bachelor's and master's program)

> Safety Science
> Science, Technology, and Globalization
> Software Engineering
> Space Physics

Master's Degree Programs

> Aeronautics
> Aerospace Engineering
> Business Administration in Aviation
> Human Factors and Systems
> Safety Science
> Software Engineering
> Space Science
> Technical Management

For More Information:

100

Embry-Riddle Aeronautical University
Daytona Beach Residential Campus
600 South Clyde Morris Boulevard
Daytona Beach, FL 32114-3900
386/226-6000
http://www.erau.edu
Degrees available: Certificates of completion
(undergraduate/graduate), bachelor's degree, master's degree

Embry-Riddle Aeronautical University
Prescott Residential Campus
3700 Willow Creek Road
Prescott, AZ 86301-3720
800/888-3728
http://www.erau.edu
Degrees available: Certificates of completion
(undergraduate/graduate), bachelor's degree, master's degree

Fun Fact

Approximately 30,000 students attend Embry-Riddle Aeronautical University.

Enology and Viticulture

Harvesting grapes, trucking them to the winery, loading them into the crushers, and supervising the aging, racking, and blending of wine is what students studying viticulture and enology experience as part of their hands-on internship experience. A select few colleges in the United States offer programs in the specialized fields of viticulture, the science of wine-grape growing, and enology, the science of wine-making. Students in these disciplines study the scientific principles that are involved in growing grapes and manufacturing wine. Degrees are available at all academic levels.

Typical Courses:

> Organic Chemistry
> Plant Propagation
> Viticulture and Small Fruits
> Chemistry and Biochemistry of Fruit and Wine
> Vineyard and Winery Systems
> Advanced Horticultural Crop Physiology
> Viticulture-Enology Interface
> Varietal wines (international and domestic)
> Winery production practices
> Must and wine analysis

Potential Employers:

> Wineries
> Distribution and retail businesses

Available At:

University of California-Davis
Department of Viticulture and Enology
One Shields Avenue
1023 Wickson Hall
Davis, CA 95616-8749
530/752-0380
http://wineserver.ucdavis.edu/content.php?category=Academics
Degrees available: Bachelor's degree, master's degree

University of California-Fresno
Department of Viticulture and Enology

Did You Know?

There are more than 3,000 wineries in the United States, according to the American Wine Society. Approximately 556,000 people work in wine-related careers in the United States.

2360 East Barstow, MS VR89
Fresno, CA 93740-8003
559/278-2089
http://cast.csufresno.edu/ve/index.htm
Degrees available: Certificate, bachelor's degree, master's degree

Shawnee Community College
8364 Shawnee College Road
Ullin, IL 62992
618/634-3216
http://www.shawneecc.edu/courses/viticulture.asp
http://www.shawneecc.edu/courses/enology_asst.asp
Degrees available: Certificate (one-year program in viticulture and one-year program in enology)

Viticulture and Enology Science and Technology Alliance
Missouri State University-Mountain Grove
9740 Red Spring Road
Mountain Grove, MO 65711-2229
417/926-4105
http://vesta-usa.org
Degrees available: Certificate, associate degree
This is a partnership between Missouri State University, Northeast Iowa Community College, Shawnee Community College in Illinois, and the Mid-America Viticulture and Enology Center, along with state agricultural agencies, to create a collaborative program of study in the fields of viticulture and enology.

Walla Walla Community College
Walla Walla Institute for Enology and Viticulture
500 Tausick Way
Walla Walla, WA 99362
509/524-5175
http://www.wwcc.edu/programs/proftech/wine/index.cfm
Degrees available: Certificate, associate degree

University of Washington
Department of Horticulture and Landscape Architecture
PO Box 646414
Pullman, WA 99164-6414
509/335-9502
http://www.wineducation.wsu.edu/curriculum.htm
Degrees available: Certificate (two-year programs), bachelor's
degree

For More Information:

American Society for Enology and Viticulture
PO Box 1855
Davis, CA 95617-1855
530/753-3142
society@asev.org
http://www.asev.org

American Wine Society
PO Box 3330
Durham, NC 27702
919/403-0022
http://www.americanwinesociety.com

Fun Fact

Wine grapes are grown in more than 40 U.S. states, according
to the American Wine Society.

Entertainment Engineering

Heart-pounding roller coaster rides. Death-defying magic shows. Awe-inspiring stage productions in which actors seem to fly through the air or walk on water. Captivated by the spectacle of Las Vegas and Broadway shows, few people stop to think about the professionals who are responsible for creating and engineering these exciting extravaganzas. But as high-tech entertainment has grown in popularity, colleges have begun to focus on training students in the new field of entertainment engineering, which combines training in engineering and theater. Professors from these two departments at the University of Nevada-Las Vegas have been working for several years to create a major in entertainment engineering. The University currently offers a minor in entertainment engineering and will offer a major in the field by 2008.

Typical Courses:

> Introduction to Engineering
> Mechanical Engineering
> Electrical Engineering
> Mathematics
> Physics
> Introduction to Stage Production

Potential Employers

> Entertainment design companies (especially in Las Vegas and Los Angeles)
> Amusement parks
> Motion picture industry
> Theaters

Available At:

University of Nevada-Las Vegas
Howard R. Hughes College of Engineering
UNLV Box 454027
Las Vegas, NV 89154-4027
http://www.unlv.edu/programs/entertech
Degrees available: Undergraduate minor currently available; bachelor's degree to be available in 2008

For More Information:

American Society for Engineering Education
1818 N Street, NW, Suite 600
Washington, DC 20036-2479
202/331-3500
http://www.asee.org

Junior Engineering Technical Society, Inc.
1420 King Street, Suite 405
Alexandria, VA 22314
703/548-5387
info@jets.org
http://www.jets.org

Interview: Robert Boehm

The editors of *They Teach That in College!?* spoke with Dr.
Robert Boehm, Distinguished Professor of Mechanical
Engineering, at the University of Nevada-Las Vegas about the
University's entertainment engineering program.

105

Q. What is entertainment engineering?

A. Entertainment engineering is not a precisely defined term. Our
definition has two elements to it, one quite general that guides
the program overall, and a more specific one that is the focus of
the early phases of our program. Overall, it is the application of
technical concepts to enhance entertainment experiences. In this
form, it could be a variety of thrusts from computer games to
live entertainment experiences. We have focused on the latter in
the initial phases of our program, in no small part because of the
high amount of related business activity in the Las Vegas area.

Q. Please briefly describe your program.

A. We are emphasizing live entertainment experiences. These can
include theatrical productions, robotic presentations, and thrill
rides. The program is being initiated next spring as a minor
that a student can attach to almost any major. We anticipate
that most of the students will be from technical theater and
engineering backgrounds.

Q. What types of skills will be taught in your program?

A. We will try to develop a way of thinking that is broader then either engineering or technical theater, so that students can create outside their normal "boxes." The program will introduce students to the basics of technical theater, key aspects of engineering, and modern applications of pertinent technology. A major emphasis of the program will immerse students in multidisciplinary design experiences. Another aspect is to bring to their attention all of the real features of the business, including traditionally short deadlines, incompletely defined concept requests that they must more fully define, and selling to the client. This will be accomplished through the use of class projects, interaction with faculty and practitioners, behind-the-scenes examination of design and operation of systems, and many formal presentations.

Q. Who will hire students from your program?

A. Many entertainment design companies, a majority of them small-sized, operate in Las Vegas and the nearby Los Angeles area. Several of these have a worldwide market. We have worked closely with many of these companies, and all have been very supportive of this thrust. Several of our students are serving in either part-time or full-time jobs with some of these companies.

Q. Do any other schools offer a similar program? If so, how will your program be different?

A. Several schools emphasize computer applications related to entertainment. Others offer programs that examine the technical aspects of filmmaking. Finally, some programs are offered that emphasize the technical aspects of technical theater. Few offer a formal melding of engineering with the fine arts in a way that emphasizes the technology in live entertainment venues.

Equestrian Studies

According to a recent study by the American Horse Council, the equine industry adds $102 billion to our economy and offers more than 1.4 million full-time jobs. Colleges have responded to our love of all things equine by creating a variety of equestrian studies programs. Majors may include equine administration or equine business, which offer training for people who are interested in becoming instructors, trainers, equine managers, riders, equine insurance adjusters, bloodstock agents, race track administrators, farm managers, and equine product salespersons, and Equestrian Science, which offers training to those interested in becoming trainers, equine managers, instructors, and riders.

Typical Courses:

> Anatomy, Movement, and Farrier Methods
> Theory of Equine Nutrition
> Stable Management
> Equine Care
> Equine Health and First Aid
> Techniques of Horse Management
> Horse Industry Overview
> Horse Show and Event Management
> Entrepreneurship
> Principles of Management

Potential Employers:

> Racetracks
> Stables
> Breeding and racing organizations
> Sales industry
> Insurance industry

Available At:

The following list of schools offering programs in equestrian studies is not exhaustive. For a complete list of programs, visit http://www.horseschools.com.

Ellsworth Community College
1100 College Avenue
Iowa Falls, IA 50126
800/322-9235
http://www.iavalley.cc.ia.us/Catalog05-06/VocTech/
VTEquineManagement.htm
Degrees available: Associate degree

University of Louisville
Equine Industry Program
College of Business and Public Administration
Louisville, KY 40292
502/852-7617
http://cbpa.louisville.edu/eip
Degrees available: Bachelor's degree, postgraduate certificate

Morehead State University
Department of Agricultural and Human Sciences
325 Reed Hall
Morehead, KY 40351
606/783-2662
http://www.moreheadstate.edu/ahs/index.aspx?id=2772
Degrees available: Bachelor's degree

University of Nebraska-Lincoln
Nebraska College of Technical Agriculture
Rural Route 3, PO Box 23A
Curtis, NE 69025
800/3CURTIS
ncta2@unl.edu
http://ncta.unl.edu/MAJORS/Aps/equine_industry_management.htm
Degrees available: Bachelor's degree

State University of New York
College of Agriculture and Technology
Marshall Hall
Morrisville, NY 13408
315/684-6083
admissions@morrisville.edu
http://www.morrisville.edu/Academics/Ag_NRC/Equine_Science
Degrees available: Associate degree, bachelor's degree

Northeastern Junior College
Equine Management Program
100 College Drive
Sterling, CO 80751

970/522-6931
http://www.njc.edu/agriculture/equinemgmt.html
Degrees available: Associate degree

Sul Ross State University
Department of Animal Science
PO Box C-11
Alpine, TX 79832
432/837-8210
http://www.sulross.edu/pages/3232.asp
Degrees available: Master's degree

Truman State University
Department of Agricultural Science
58 Barnett Hall
Kirksville, MO 63501
660/785-4584
http://agriculture.truman.edu/areas%20of%20study/equine.htm
Degrees available: Bachelor's degree

William Woods University
One University Avenue
Fulton, MO 65251
800/995-3159
http://www.williamwoods.edu
Degrees available: Bachelor's degree

For More Information:

American Horse Council
1616 H Street, NW, 7th Floor
Washington, DC 20006
202/296-4031
AHC@horsecouncil.org
http://www.horsecouncil.org

American Riding Instructors Association
28801 Trenton Court
Bonita Springs, FL 34134-3337
239/948-3232
aria@riding-instructor.com
http://www.riding-instructor.com

American Youth Horse Council
800/879-2942
info@ayhc.com
http://www.ayhc.com

Fashion Design

Are you obsessed with the latest fashions? Do you have a creative side that manifests itself in the unique clothes you wear? If so, perhaps a career in the fast-paced world of fashion design would be a perfect fit. But, don't be fooled into thinking fashion design is all glamour and no work. The recent Tommy Hilfiger-hosted fashion reality television show, *The Cut,* proved how cutthroat the world of fashion design can be. However, there is plenty of room for professionals in the industry who don't attain pop star-like fame by creating their own lines of clothing. A degree in fashion design prepares students to work as designers, pattern makers, illustrators, fabric buyers, sewers, and sample makers, and each of these positions plays a vital role in the developmental process of creating a line of clothing. Individuals well suited for careers in fashion design are those who thrive under pressure, are resourceful, original thinkers, and enjoy some level of risk taking. Fashion design degrees are available at all academic levels.

Typical Courses:

> Concept Development
> Drawing Fundamentals
> 3D Design
> Fashion History, Culture, and Society
> Fashion Drawing
> Computer-Aided Design
> Shoe Design
> Studio Methods
> Current Issues in the Global Fashion Industry
> Flat Pattern/Draping

Potential Employers:

> Fashion studio owners
> Textile and apparel manufacturers
> Retailers
> Department stores
> Fashion magazines and other publications
> Fashion houses

Available At:

The following list of schools offering programs in fashion design is not exhaustive. For a complete list of programs, visit the following website, http://fashionschools.com.

Ball State University
Department of Family and Consumer Sciences
150 Applied Technology Building
Muncie, IN 47306
765/285-5931
http://www.bsu.edu/fcs/article/0,,10242—,00.html
Degrees available: Bachelor's degree, master's degree

Fashion Institute of Technology
Seventh Avenue at 27th Street, Building B, Room 701
New York, NY 10001-5992
212/217-7667
fitinfo@fitnyc.edu
http://www.fitnyc.edu/aspx/Content.aspx?menu=Future:Schools
AndPrograms:ArtAndDesign:FashionDesign
Degrees available: Associate degree, bachelor's degree

Houston Community College-Central College
1300 Holman, PO Box 7849
Houston, TX 77270-7849
713/718-6152
http://www.hccs.edu/discipline/Fshd/fshd.html
Degrees available: Certificate, associate degree

Kent State University
The Fashion School
PO Box 5190
Kent, OH 44242-0001
330/672-3010
erhodes1@kent.edu
http://www.fashionschool.kent.edu/majors.htm
Degrees available: Bachelor's degree

University of North Carolina
School of Human Environmental Sciences
210 Stone Building
336/334-5250
Greensboro, NC 27402-6170
http://www.uncg.edu/reg/Catalog/current/CRS/intro.html
Degrees available: Bachelor's degree

Oklahoma State University
Department of Design, Housing, and Merchandising
101 HES
Stillwater, OK 74078
405/744-5053
http://www.ches.okstate.edu/DHM/Degree_Programs/
undergrad_degree_programs.html
Degrees available: Bachelor's degree

Oregon State University
College of Health and Human Sciences
123 Women's Building
Corvallis, OR 97331-5109
541/737-3220
hhs@oregonstate.edu
http://www.hhs.oregonstate.edu/dhe/undergraduate/
apparel-design.html
Degrees available: Bachelor's degree, master's degree

Otis College of Art and Design
Fashion Design Program
9045 Lincoln Boulevard
Los Angeles, CA 90045
310/665 6875
fashion@otis.edu
http://www.otis.edu
Degrees available: Bachelor's degree

Parsons The New School for Design
560 7th Avenue
New York, NY 10011
212/229-8989
studentinfo@newschool.edu
http://www.parsons.edu/departments/
department.aspx?dID=73&sdID=96&pType=1
Degrees available: Bachelor's degree

Philadelphia University
School of Engineering and Textiles
School House Lane & Henry Avenue
Philadelphia, PA 19144
215/951-2750
http://www.philau.edu/FashionDesign
Degrees available: Certificate, bachelor's degree

Santa Ana College
1530 West 17th Street
Santa Ana, CA 92706-3398
714/564-6000
http://www.sac.edu/degrees/sac/
Fashion_Design_and_Custom_Clothing.htm
Degrees available: Certificate, associate degree

Santa Monica College
Fashion Design and Merchandising Department
1900 Pico Boulevard
Santa Monica, CA 90405
310/434-4000
http://homepage.smc.edu/mobasheri_fereshteh/fm
Degrees available: Certificate, associate degree

Stephens College
Department of Design and Fashion
Campus Box 2121
Columbia, MO 65215
800/876-7207
info@stephens.edu
http://www.stephens.edu/academics/programs/fashion
Degrees available: Bachelor's degree

University of Wisconsin-Stout
320 Home Economics Building
Menomonie, WI 54751-0790
715/232-1194
http://www.uwstout.edu/programs/bsadd
Degrees available: Bachelor's degree

For More Information:

American Apparel and Footwear Association
1601 North Kent Street, Suite 1200
Arlington, VA 22209
800/520-2262
http://www.americanapparel.org

Fashion Group International, Inc.
8 West 40th Street, 7th Floor
New York, NY 10018
212/302-5511
info@fgi.org
http:\\www.fgi.org

International Association of Clothing Designers and Executives
124 West 93rd Street, Suite 3E
New York, NY 10025
212/222-2082
newyorkiacde@nyc.rr.com
http://www.iacde.com

National Association of Schools of Art and Design
11250 Roger Bacon Drive, Suite 21
Reston, VA 20190-5248
703/437-0700
info@arts-accredit.org
http://nasad.arts-accredit.org

Careerthreads.com
http://www.careerthreads.com

Council of Fashion Designers of America
http://www.cfda.com

Fashion Merchandising and Management

If last winter's hottest trend was tucking your jeans into colorful, furry boots, no doubt this winter it will be a fashion no-no. Yet, 10 years from now, the look may reappear—with a new twist. Black is in. Brown is out. Flats are in, heels are out. The world of fashion is indeed one of constant, evolutionary change. The "business" behind the "trends" is no different. Those who enter the field are generally those who strive to always stay a step ahead of the crowd with the latest styles. They have an aptitude for business and people, and a sincere dedication to a career that promises to never become stagnant! Students' studies will focus on the areas of retailing, merchandising, marketing, and management. They'll explore topics such as consumer influence, global economics, and emerging technology, as they relate to the business of fashion. Professionals with degrees in fashion merchandising may become managers of stores, departments or areas within stores, or groups of stores. Others go on to manage special events such as fashion shows, design store window displays, or purchase lines of clothing for department stores. Entrepreneurial minded students open their own boutiques. Degrees in fashion merchandising and management are available at all academic levels.

Typical Courses:
> Clothing Adornment and Human Behavior
> Textile and Apparel Economics
> Textile Science
> Merchandising Promotion
> Merchandising Systems
> Social-Psychological Aspects of Clothing
> Historic Textiles
> Retail Sales and Customer Strategies

Potential Employers:
> Retailers
> Wholesalers

Available At:

The following list of schools offering programs in fashion merchandising and management is not exhaustive. For a complete list of programs, visit http://fashionschools.com.

Ball State University
Department of Family and Consumer Sciences
150 Applied Technology Building
Muncie, IN 47306
765/285-5931
aspangle@bsu.edu
http://www.bsu.edu/fcs/article/0,1894,35151-4865-10249,00.html
Degrees available: Bachelor's degree, master's degree

California State Polytechnic University
Merchandising and Managing Department
3801 West Temple Avenue
Pomona, CA 91768
909/869-4772
http://www.csupomona.edu/~amm
Degrees available: Bachelor's degree

Central Missouri State University
PO Box 800
Warrensburg, MO 64093
660/543-4861
http://www.cmsu.edu/x72719.xml
Degrees available: Bachelor's degree

Houston Community College-Central College
1300 Holman, PO Box 7849
Houston, TX 77004
713/718-6152
http://www.hccs.edu/discipline/Fshn/fshn.html
Degrees available: Certificate, associate degree

Kent State University
The Fashion School
PO Box 5190
Kent, OH 44242-0001
330/672-3010
erhodes1@kent.edu
http://www.fashionschool.kent.edu/majors.htm
Degrees available: Bachelor's degree, master's degree

University of Missouri-Columbia
Department of Textile and Apparel Management
137 Stanley Hall
Columbia, MO 65211
573/882-6316
http://www.missouri.edu/%7Etam
Degrees available: Bachelor's degree, master's degree, doctorate
degree

University of North Carolina
Textile Products Design and Marketing
210 Stone Building, PO Box 26170
Greensboro, NC 27402-6170
336/334-5250
TDM@uncg.edu
http://www.uncg.edu/tdm/tdm_programs/graduate.html
Degrees available: Bachelor's degree, master's degree, doctorate
degree

Oregon State University

College of Health and Human Sciences
123 Women's Building
Corvallis, OR 97331-5109
541/737-3220
hhs@oregonstate.edu
http://www.hhs.oregonstate.edu/dhe/undergraduate/
merchandising.html
Degrees available: Bachelor's degree, master's degree

Philadelphia University
School of Business Administration
School House Lane & Henry Avenue
Philadelphia, PA 19144
215/951-2827
http://www.philau.edu/sba/undergradmajors/Fash_Merch
Degrees available: Bachelor's degree, master's degree

University of Rhode Island
Department of Textiles, Fashion Merchandising, and Design
55 Lower College Road
Kingston, RI 02881
401/874-4574
http://www.uri.edu/hss/tmd
Degrees available: Bachelor's degree, master's degree, post-baccalaureate certificate

Sam Houston State University
Department of Family and Consumer Sciences
PO Box 2177
Huntsville, TX 77341
936/294-1242
hcc_fcs@shsu.edu
http://www.shsu.edu/~hec_www/degree-prog.html
Degrees available: Bachelor's degree

Santa Ana College
1530 West 17th Street
Santa Ana, CA 92706-3398
714/564-6000
http://www.sac.edu/degrees/sac/Fashion_Merchandising.htm
Degrees available: Certificate, associate degree

Santa Monica College
Fashion Design and Merchandising Department
1900 Pico Boulevard
Santa Monica, CA 90405
310/434-4000
http://homepage.smc.edu/mobasheri_fereshteh/fm
Degrees available: Associate degree

University of Wisconsin-Stout
281D Technology Wing, Jarvis Hall
Menomonie, WI 54751-0790
715/232-1365
magliok@uwstout.edu
http://www.uwstout.edu/programs/bsrmm
Degrees available: Bachelor's degree

For More Information:

American Apparel and Footwear Association
1601 North Kent Street, Suite 1200
Arlington, VA 22209
800/520-2262
http://www.apparelandfootwear.org

American Purchasing Society
PO Box 256
Aurora, IL 60506
630/859-0250
http://www.american-purchasing.com

International Association of Clothing Designers and Executives
124 West 93rd Street, Suite 3E
New York, NY 10025
212/222-2082
newyorkiacde@nyc.rr.com
http://www.iacde.com

National Retail Federation
325 7th Street, NW, Suite 1100
Washington, DC 20004
800/673-4692
http://www.nrf.com/content/
default.asp?folder=foundation&file=main.htm&bhcp=1

Careerthreads.com
http://www.careerthreads.com

Interview: Jean Gipe

Professor Jean Gipe is the Interim Chair of the Apparel
Merchandising & Management Department at California State
Polytechnic University in Pomona, California. Professor Gipe
discussed her program and the education of fashion students
with the editors of *They Teach That in College!?*

Q. Please provide a brief overview of your program.

A. The Apparel Merchandising and Management (AMM) degree
prepares students for professional positions in the apparel
and textile complex. AMM students learn about the business
of fashion (and related sewn products), which includes manufacturing, wholesaling, and retailing. Students take courses
in fashion, business, and engineering to be prepared for
supervisory and management-level positions.

Q. What high school subjects/activities should students
focus on to be successful in this major?

A. Students who complete a college preparatory program with
strong math skills and computer skills will be best prepared.
Art courses are recommended for those interested in the creative side of the business.

Q. What are the most important personal and professional qualities for fashion merchandising/management majors?

A. We recommend students look for a career that they have a passion for, and most of our AMM students really enjoy everything about fashion. The fashion industry is high energy, fast paced, all about change, and "beating the clock." The environment is all about delivering great product to a target customer and making money in the process.

Some of the positions in the industry are very analytical, requiring excellent management/organizational skills. Other positions are more creative, requiring an eye for design and style and an understanding of what would appeal to the customer.

Q. How will the field of fashion merchandising/management change in the future?

A. Technology will continue to change the industry. Time is money and technology continues to remove wasted time from the process of doing business. While the apparel industry has always been a global industry, enhanced technology will require stronger management skills to do an ever increasing volume of business at a distance.

Interview: Linda Welters

Dr. Linda Welters is the Chairperson of the Department of Textiles, Fashion Merchandising and Design at the University of Rhode Island, which is located in Kingston, Rhode Island. She was kind enough to discuss her program and the education of fashion students with the editors of *They Teach That in College!?*

Q. Please provide a brief overview of your program.

A. The University of Rhode Island offers two programs leading to the Bachelor of Science; the first is Textiles, Fashion Merchandising and Design (TMD), and the second is Textile Marketing. We also offer a Master of Science in Textiles, Fashion Merchandising and Design.

The TMD degree prepares students for a wide variety of careers in fashion or interior design, fashion merchandising, or textile science. The program is designed for students who want a university degree rather than a degree from a technical school or a design school. Students take general education courses in addition to a set of core courses in the major that educate them about textile materials and the manufacturing, merchandising, and retailing of fashion products. Fashion today is a competitive, global field. Many of our students study abroad in England, France, Italy, or Australia. Many complete internships with major fashion companies both at the wholesale level (e.g., Giorgio Armani) and the retail level (e.g., Nordstrom). Students must complete 18 credits of professional electives; often these are art or business courses. This program offers the flexibility to pursue interests in one of four areas: fashion design, interior design, textile science (yes, our students are required to take chemistry), and merchandising (both micro- and macro-economics are required).

121

The Textile Marketing major provides students with a focused background for marketing textile and fashion products. This program is highly structured, combining courses in consumer, cultural, business, and scientific aspects to textiles and fashion with courses from the College of Business Administration in quantitative business skills, accounting, business law, marketing, and management. The courses covers planning, selling, pricing, promotion, and distribution of textile products. It prepares students for careers in corporate sales, buying, and quality control.

The Master's degree has three tracks: Textile Science, Historic Textiles/Dress, and Fashion Merchandising. These students focus on latest scholarship in their chosen area in order to conduct research and produce a thesis. The students produce high-quality work that is presented at professional conferences and published in scientific journals.

In addition, we have a fashion merchandising society that orchestrates a fashion show every spring of students' own designs, a Textile Gallery that features changing exhibitions of artifacts from our extensive Historic Textile and Costume Collection (current exhibition is "Nature's Dyes: Textile from Around the Globe"), and we offer a winter study tour to London and Paris.

Q. What high school subjects/activities should students focus on to be successful in this major?

A. Math, chemistry, art. Any club/group where students can show leadership potential is good. I also advocate working in fashion retail. No matter what area of fashion a student may end up in, knowing consumer behavior is critical to success.

Q. What are the most important personal and professional qualities for fashion merchandising majors?

A. They must enjoy a fast-paced, constantly changing environment (e.g., adapt well to change) and they must be outgoing, friendly, and communicate well.

Q. How will the field of fashion merchandising, and fashion in general, change in the future?

A. The field is constantly changing. As previously mentioned, the fashion industry is global. China is manufacturing more and more of the products sold in developed countries. In cooperation with the Languages Department, we have a proposal here at the University of Rhode Island that would bring a full-time Chinese language instructor to campus. Some of our majors should learn Chinese so that they can travel there to work directly with the factories. Our spring seminar this year is "Made in China"; it will explore the history, demographics, culture, and manufacturing capability of this powerful country.

Another important feature of the field's future is the need for technological and design innovation. The U.S., Europe, and Japan lead the world in developing innovative products. We need to develop talent that continues to be innovative.

Forensic Science

If the terms DNA, body decay, blood splatter, and rigor mortis fascinate rather than repulse you, you might have a future in the forensic sciences. Popularized by television shows such as *CSI: Crime Scene Investigation, Crossing Jordan,* and *The X Files,* the forensic sciences are enjoying remarkable popularity on college campuses. The American Academy of Forensic Sciences reports that there are five associate and certificate programs, 18 bachelor's degree programs, 22 master's degree programs, and at least two Ph.D. programs in forensic science in the United States. Degrees (at all academic levels) are available in the following concentrations: Forensic Science, Forensic Psychology, Forensic and Toxicological Chemistry, Forensic and Investigative Science, Forensic DNA Profiling, Forensic Anthropology, Forensic Biology, Forensic Pathology, and Forensic Accounting. No formal accreditation system exists for these programs. The National Institute of Justice, a branch of the Justice Department, is working to develop standards that may eventually result in a voluntary accreditation system. In the meanwhile, those interested in forensic science should be sure to carefully investigate programs of interest before enrolling.

Typical Courses:

> Crime Scene Investigation
> Forensic Anthropology
> Survey of Forensic Science
> Death Investigation
> Firearms Evidence
> Forensic Entomology
> Medical Terminology
> Human Physiology
> Laboratory Measurements and Techniques
> Organic Chemistry
> Forensic Chemistry
> Biochemistry
> Statistics for Biomedical Sciences
> Criminology

Potential Employers:

> State and local law enforcement agencies

> Government agencies (i.e., the Drug Enforcement
>   Administration; the Bureau of Alcohol, Tobacco, Firearms, and
>   Explosives; the Federal Bureau of Investigation; the United
>   States Postal Service; the Secret Service; the Central Intelligence
>   Agency; and United States Fish and Wildlife Services)
> Hospitals
> Medical schools
> Medical examiners

Available At:

The following list of colleges that offer degrees in forensic science is
not exhaustive. Visit the American Academy of Forensic Sciences
website (http://www.aafs.org) for a complete list of colleges and universities that offer programs in forensic science.

Anne Arundel Community College
101 College Parkway
Arnold, MD 21012-1895
410/777-AACC
http://www.aacc.edu/criminaljustice/ForensicScience.cfm
Degrees available: Associate degree

Baylor University
Forensic Science Program
Department of Sociology
PO Box 97370
Waco, TX 76798
http://www.baylor.edu/forensic_science
Degrees available: Bachelor's degree

University of California-Davis
Graduate Group in Forensic Science
1333 Research Park Drive
Davis, CA 95616
530/757-8878
forensic@unexmail.ucdavis.edu
http://www.extension.ucdavis.edu/forensics
Degrees available: Master's degree

Chaminade University of Honolulu
Forensic Sciences Program
3140 Waialae Avenue
Honolulu, HI 96816-1578
808/440-4209

http://www.chaminade.edu/csi/
index.php?pg=content_CUH_FS.html
Degrees available: Bachelor's degree

George Washington University
Department of Forensic Sciences
2036 H Street, Samson Hall
Washington, DC 20052
202/994-7319
forsc@gwu.edu
http://www.gwu.edu/~forensic
Degrees available: Master's degree

Grossmont Community College
8800 Grossmont College Drive
El Cajon, CA 92020
619/644-7000
http://www.grossmont.edu/aoj/forensic.asp
Degrees available: Associate degree

John Jay College of Criminal Justice
899 Tenth Avenue
New York, NY 10019
212/237-8000
http://www.jjay.cuny.edu
Degrees available: Bachelor's degree, master's degree, doctorate
degree

Michigan State University
Forensic Science Program
School of Criminal Justice
560A Baker Hall
East Lansing, MI 48824
517/353-7133
forsci@msu.edu
http://www.forensic.msu.edu
Degrees available: Master's degree

University of North Dakota
Forensic Science Program
PO Box 8374
Grand Forks, ND 58202-8374
701/777-3008
forensic@und.nodak.edu
http://www.und.edu/dept/forensic
Degrees available: Bachelor's degree

Oklahoma State University
Center for Health Sciences
Graduate Program in Forensic Sciences
1111 West 17th Street
Tulsa, OK 74107
918/582-1972
http://www.healthsciences.okstate.edu/forensic/index.htm
Degrees available: Master's degree

West Virginia University
Forensic Program
PO Box 6121
Morgantown, WV 26506
304/293-2453
forensicinfo@mail.wvu.edu
http://www.wvu.edu/~forensic
Degrees available: Bachelor's degree

For More Information:

American Academy of Forensic Sciences
PO Box 669
Colorado Springs, CO 80901-0669
719/636-1100
http://www.aafs.org

Society of Forensic Toxicologists
PO Box 5543
Mesa, AZ 85211-5543
480/839-9106
http://www.soft-tox.org

Franklin W. Olin College of Engineering

The Franklin W. Olin College of Engineering in Needham , Massachusetts, is an innovative engineering college "that bridges science and technology, enterprise, and society . . . via an interdisciplinary, project-based approach emphasizing entrepreneurship, liberal arts, and rigorous science and engineering fundamentals." Olin seeks to prepare graduates to think creatively and be more innovative as they address today's engineering challenges. This institution is highly selective, but those who are admitted receive four-year, full tuition scholarships worth approximately $130,000. The College has more than 35 clubs and campus organizations, including Butterfingers Club (juggling), *Frankly Speaking* (student newspaper), Jazz Orchestra, and Olin Entrepreneurial Group. The College has a 9 to 1 student/faculty ratio.

Available Fields of Study:

The College, which was founded in 2002, offers undergraduate programs in Electrical and Computer Engineering, Mechanical Engineering, and Engineering (concentrations in BioEngineering, Computing, Materials Science, and Systems). Due to the interdisciplinary nature of the College, there are no separate academic departments.

For More Information:

Franklin W. Olin College of Engineering
Olin Way
Needham, MA 02492-1200
781/292-2300
info@olin.edu
http://www.olin.edu/on.asp
Degrees available: Bachelor's degree

Gaming Industry

Casinos are found not just in Las Vegas and Atlantic City anymore; they are popping up throughout the United States. Whether you love or hate casinos, it is clear that the gaming industry is playing an increasing role in the health of local economies across the United States. In addition to gambling entities on Native American reservations, commercial casinos can be found in Colorado, Illinois, Indiana, Iowa, Louisiana, Michigan, Mississippi, Missouri, Nevada, New Jersey, and South Dakota. Although educational requirements vary by casino, our nation's colleges are beginning to recognize the demand for training in "gambling-ology." Certificates and degrees are available in casino management, tribal gaming, and other areas.

Typical Courses:

> Introduction to Gaming Management
> Gaming Device Management
> Surveillance and Security
> Casino Industry Regulation
> Casino Resort Management Food and Beverage
> Marketing
> Mathematics and Statistics
> Introduction to Indian Gaming

Potential Employers:

> Commercial casinos
> Native American casinos

Available At:

Grossmont College
8800 Grossmont College Drive
El Cajon, CA 92020-1799
http://www.grossmont.edu
Degrees available: Certificate, associate degree

Mohave Community College
1971 Jagerson Avenue
Kingman, AZ 86401
http://www.mohave.edu/pages/1455.asp
Degrees available: Certificate, associate degree

Fun Fact

More than 54.1 million Americans visited a casino in 2004, according to a Harrah's Entertainment poll.

University of Nevada-Las Vegas
College of Hotel Administration
4505 Maryland Parkway, Box 456013
Las Vegas, NV 89154-6013
http://hotel.unlv.edu/departGameMgt.html
Degrees available: Bachelor's degree

Northeast Wisconsin Technical College
2740 West Mason Street, PO Box 19042
Green Bay, WI 54307-9042
http://www.nwtc.tec.wi.us
Degrees available: Associate degree

San Diego State University
College of Extended Studies
5250 Campanile Drive
San Diego, CA 92182
http://www.ces.sdsu.edu/casino.html
Degrees available: Certificate

Tulane University
A. B. Freeman School of Business
125 Gibson Hall
New Orleans, LA 70118
www.tulane.edu/~choose/new_page_8.htm
Degrees available: Associate degree, post-baccalaureate certificate

For More Information:

American Gaming Association
555 13th Street, NW, Suite 1010 East
Washington, DC 20004-1109
http://www.americangaming.org

National Indian Gaming Association
224 2nd Street, SE
Washington, DC 20003
http://www.indiangaming.org

Golf Course Management

The work of golf course managers is not all fun and games. These key professionals in the golf industry must be expert marketers, merchandisers, accountants, managers, and event planners, as well able to handle the more technical aspects of the career such as golf course maintenance and golf club repair. Degree programs in professional golf management offer interdisciplinary curriculums in business, general studies, recreation and tourism management, and golf that prepare graduates for successful careers. The Professional Golfers' Association of America (PGA) Professional Golf Management University Program, a four-and-a-half-year college curriculum for aspiring PGA professionals, is offered at 17 PGA-accredited colleges and universities nationwide.

Typical Courses:

> Tournament Operations and the Rules of Golf
> Facility Operations
> Turfgrass Management
> Fundamentals of Golf Instruction
> Managerial Accounting
> Principles of Marketing
> Economics
> Business Information Systems
> Small Business Management
> Golf Internships

Did You Know?

Golf was invented in Scotland in the 1500s.

Potential Employers:

> Golf courses
> Golf equipment manufacturers
> Colleges and universities
> Resorts

Available At:

Arizona State University
Morrison School of Agribusiness and Resource Management
7001 East Williams Field Road, Building #20
Mesa, AZ 85212

http://www.east.asu.edu/msabr/pgm
Degrees available: Bachelor's degree

Campbell University
Lundy-Fetterman School of Business
PO Box 218
Buies Creek, NC 27506
800/334-4111, ext. 1395
http://www.campbell.edu/catalog/current/pgm.html
Degrees available: Bachelor's degree

Clemson University
Parks, Recreation and Tourism Management Department
282-A Lehotsky Hall
Clemson, SC 29634
864/656-2230
http://www.hehd.clemson.edu/PRTM/PGM
Degrees available: Bachelor's degree

Coastal Carolina University
Wall College of Business
PO Box 261954
Conway, SC 29528-6054
843/347-3161
http://www.coastal.edu/business
Degrees available: Bachelor's degree

University of Colorado-Colorado Springs
College of Business
1420 Austin Bluffs Parkway
PO Box 7150
Colorado Springs, CO 80933-7150
800/990-8227
http://business.uccs.edu/pgm
Degrees available: Bachelor's degree

Ferris State University
School of Business
1506 Knollview Drive
Big Rapids, MI 49307
231/591-2380
PGM@ferris.edu
http://www.ferris.edu/htmls/colleges/business/pgm
Degrees available: Bachelor's degree

Florida Gulf Coast University
Department of Resort and Hospitality Management
10501 FGCU Boulevard South
Fort Myers, FL 33965-6565
800/590-3428
http://cps.fgcu.edu/resort
Degrees available: Bachelor's degree

Florida State University
Professional Golf Management
2550 Pottsdamer Street
Tallahassee, FL 32306-2581
850/644-0213
http://www.cob.fsu.edu/dsh/pgm_major.cfm
Degrees available: Bachelor's degree

University of Idaho
College of Business and Economics
Professional Golf Management Program
PO Box 443161
Moscow, ID 83844-3161
208/885-4746
http://www.uidaho.edu/pgm/program.html
Degrees available: Bachelor's degree

Methodist College
5400 Ramsey Street
Fayetteville, NC 28311
800/488-7110, ext. 7278
http://www.methodist.edu/pgm/index.htm
Degrees available: Bachelor's degree

Mississippi State University
College of Business and Industry
104 McCool Hall, PO Box 5288
Mississippi State, MS 39762
662/325-3161
http://misweb.cbi.msstate.edu/~COBI/faculty/departments/
mainpage.shtml?PGM
Degrees available: Bachelor's degree

University of Nebraska-Lincoln
225 Keim Hall
Lincoln, NE 68583-7467
402/472-7467
pgm@unl.edu

http://pgm.unl.edu
Degrees available: Bachelor's degree

University of Nevada-Las Vegas (UNLV)
UNLV Harrah Hotel College
4505 Maryland Parkway, PO Box 6023
Las Vegas, NV 89154-6023
702/895-2932
http://hotel.unlv.edu/PGM.htm
Degrees available: Bachelor's degree

New Mexico State University
PO Box 30001, Department PGM
Las Cruces, NM 88003
505/646-2814
http://pgm.nmsu.edu
Degrees available: Bachelor's degree

North Carolina State University
Campus Box 7103
Raleigh, NC 27695-7103
http://natural-resources.ncsu.edu:8100/pgm
Degrees available: Bachelor's degree

Penn State University
University Park, PA 16802
814/863-8987
http://www.psu.edu/admissions/steps/understanding/
addreq.htm#golf
Degrees available: Bachelor's degree

Sam Houston State University
PO Box 2056
Huntsville, TX 77341-2056
936/294-4810
rmb002@shsu.edu
http://www.shsu.edu
Degrees available: Bachelor's degree

For More Information:

Golf Course Superintendents Association of America
1421 Research Park Drive
Lawrence, KS 66049-3859
800/472-7878
infobox@gcsaa.org
http://www.gcsaa.org

Interview: Jim Riscigno

Jim Riscigno is the Director of the Professional Golf Management Program at Florida State University in Tallahassee, Florida. He discussed his program with the editors of *They Teach That in College!?*

Q. Please tell us about your program.

A. Our Professional Golf Management Major resides in our College of Business, the area of specialty is Hospitality and the major is Professional Golf Management. Our students learn about the business of golf and how the game of golf runs as a business. When our students graduate they have a Bachelor of Science Degree from a nationally ranked College of Business (the major is in the Dedman School of Hospitality, which is ranked 5th by industry), and they will be a PGA member and Class A professional. Many of our students go on to become general managers, owners, and corporate executives.

Q. What are the most important personal and professional qualities for golf course management majors?

A. They should have personality, a positive attitude, a strong service ethic, like to be with people, and like to serve others. Playing skills are also important. Students should play on their golf team and take a business-oriented curriculum.

Q. What advice would you offer golf course management majors as they graduate and look for jobs?

A. Be prepared to work hard, learn from others, and understand that this is the service and hospitality industry. Our industry is all about 'relationships' and the big winners know how important relationships are and the need to create a 'win win' environment. Focus on your strengths and what you have to offer your employer. Be realistic about your strengths, weaknesses, and work to improve both.

Homeland Security

Since the terrorist attacks of September 11, 2001, the U.S. government has had the daunting task of protecting our nation from future attacks—whether on infrastructure such as bridges, power plants, and dams; our food and water supply; civilians; or other targets. In November 2002, Congress created the Department of Homeland Security (DHS) to protect our nation from terrorist threats. In response, two- and four-year colleges have developed or expanded curriculum that aims to educate and train students to work for the DHS; other government agencies at the federal, state, and local level; and private security companies. Students in homeland security programs often have the opportunity to pursue a variety of tracks, including aviation safety and security, emergency medical services management, computer security, forensic sciences, public health and emergency management, telecommunication and national security, information security management, and computer fraud investigations. Students in each track take common core courses as well as general studies courses. Degrees in homeland security are available at the certificate, associate, baccalaureate, and master degree level.

Typical Courses:

> Aviation Security
> Airline Transport Security
> Risk Management
> Terrorism, Counter Terrorism, and Terrorism Response
> Disaster Preparedness and Emergency Systems
> Emergency Response to Terrorism
> Cyberterrorism

Potential Employers:

> State and local government agencies
> Federal government agencies (such as the Department of Homeland Security; the Bureau of Alcohol, Tobacco, Firearms, and Explosives; and the Federal Bureau of Investigation)
> Private security companies
> Hospitals
> Airports
> Amusement parks

> Cruise industry
> Rail transportation industry

Available At:

Many colleges and universities are in the process of developing programs in homeland security. Some schools offer a concentration in homeland security, usually within their criminal justice departments. Check with institutions near you to determine if majors, minors, or concentrations are available in homeland security. You can also visit http://www.training.fema.gov/EMIWeb/edu/collegelist/DHSASSOCIATE for a short list of programs.

Corinthian Colleges
714/427-3000
http://www.cci.edu/default.asp
Degrees available: Associate degree, bachelor's degree
Corinthian Colleges, Inc., one of the largest postsecondary education companies in North America, operating 96 colleges in 24 states in the U.S. and 33 colleges in seven provinces in Canada, offers degrees in Homeland Security at many of its campuses. Visit the organization's website for further information.

Fairmont State Community and Technical College
School of Health and Human Services
Homeland Security Program
315 Hardway Hall
Fairmont, WV 26554
304/367-4678
http://www.fairmontstate.edu/academics/homeland_security_overview.asp
Degrees available: Associate degree

George Washington University
2300 I Street, NW, Suite 721
Washington, DC 20037
202/994-2437
hspi@gwu.edu
http://www.homelandsecurity.gwu.edu
Degrees available: Certificate, associate degree, bachelor's degree, master's degree

Michigan State University
School of Criminal Justice
Global Community Security Institute

East Lansing, MI 48824
517/432-3156
http://homelandsecurity.msu.edu
Degrees available: Certificate (online courses only)

San Diego State University
5500 Campanile Drive
San Diego, CA 92182
http://homelandsecurity.sdsu.edu
Degrees available: Master's degree

The Ohio State University
Department of International Studies
3086 Derby Hall
154 North Oval Mall
Columbus, OH 43210-1347
614/292-9657
foster.24@osu.edu
http://homelandsecurity.osu.edu/education.html
http://psweb.sbs.ohio-state.edu/International/majors/
security_intelligence.html
Degrees available: Bachelor's degree (in International Studies
with a specialization in Security and Intelligence)

Virginia Commonwealth University
L. Douglas Wilder School of Government and Public Affairs
923 West Franklin Street
Richmond, VA 23284
804/828-8038
http://www.has.vcu.edu/gov/Programs/HMSec.html
Degrees available: Bachelor's degree

For More Information:

National Academic Consortium for Homeland Security
Program for International and Homeland Security
The Ohio State University
1501 Neil Avenue, Mershon Center
Columbus, OH 43201
614/688-3420
NACHS@osu.edu
http://homelandsecurity.osu.edu/NACHS

U.S. Department of Homeland Security
Washington, DC 20528
http://www.dhs.gov/dhspublic

Interview: Les Boggess

Fairmont State Community & Technical College in Fairmont, West Virginia, created one of the first associate degree programs in homeland security in the United States. The editors of *They Teach That in College!?* discussed the program with Les Boggess, Program Coordinator.

Q. Please briefly describe your program.

A. Our program is a multitrack degree program. A student can choose to follow either criminal justice, aviation, safety, or emergency medical services tracks. There are common core classes as well as specific courses for the track, as well as general studies courses. At present, we are offering a two-year associate degree.

Q. What types of students enter your program? What are their career goals and interests?

A. Frequently, students who enroll in this program are also enrolled in the four year Criminal Justice program. They can count the associate degree as their minor for criminal justice. Other students are planning a career strictly in homeland security, and major only in that field.

Q. What types of careers will students be able to work in upon completion of his or her degree?

A. There are all sorts of employment opportunities opening up at the federal level, but also in the private sector and among city, local, and county government agencies.

Q. What personal qualities should a student have to be successful in your program and in their post-college career?

A. Motivation, a desire to help others and be part of a team, academic discipline, and a clean police record. They must also possess integrity, be a U.S. citizen, and be able to pass a background check.

Q. Does your school have any type of relationship with the Department of Homeland Security (DHS)?

A. Yes. I attended seminars this summer with the Department of Homeland Security and maintain close contact with representatives of the DHS. Our program is listed on the website maintained at http://www.training.fema.gov/EMIWeb/edu/collegelist/dhsassociate.

Q. Is the DHS a logical career path for graduates of your program?

A. Yes. There will be many jobs created in the next few years that do not currently exist. Although it is unfortunate that these jobs are necessary, political reality suggests that we must of necessity become a more careful society, guarding against attacks both from outside and from within.

139

Industrial Distribution

Businesses in every industry have had to evolve due to globalization, but the business of industrial distribution has been markedly changed. Rapidly changing computer technology has made it possible for global competitors to provide equally fast and cost-effective distribution services to end users who are looking for the best, and least expensive, service possible. With the end-goal being to increase sales and service to a client, industrial distributors must focus on how to move their goods most cost effectively and efficiently. What once was, for all practical purposes, impossible—a company in China being able to outbid a company in the United States to distribute a product manufactured in yet another country, from point A to points B, C, and D—has made for a competitive atmosphere within the industry. As a result, highly trained, technologically savvy individuals are needed as this field continues to grow and evolve.

Typical Courses:

> Distributor Information and Control Systems
> Distributor Operations and Financial Management
> Distribution Logistics
> Manufacturer Distributor Relations
> Computer Applications in Distribution
> Purchasing Applications in Distribution
> The Quality Process for Distributors
> Distributor Customer Base Management
> Manufacturing and Assembly Processes
> Industrial Automation

Potential Employers:

> Consulting companies
> Information technology companies
> Engineering companies
> Global supply chain management companies
> Manufacturing engineering companies
> Technical sales and marketing

Available At:

The following list of colleges that offer degrees in industrial distribution programs is not exhaustive. For more schools that offer such programs, visit http://www.mrotoday.com/progressive/indlinks/schools.htm.

University of Alabama-Birmingham
School of Business
219 Business-Engineering Complex
1150 10th Avenue South
Birmingham, AL 35294-4460
205/934-8850
http://www.business.uab.edu/files/Degree_Programs/
ID_Program/ID_Program.htm
Degrees available: Bachelor's degree

University of Illinois-Urbana-Champaign
Industrial Distribution Management Program
1206 South Sixth Street
Champaign IL. 61820
217/265-0794
http://www.business.uiuc.edu/idm/
Degrees available: Bachelor's degree

University of Southern California
Department of Marketing
3670 Trousdale Parkway, BRI 103
Los Angeles, CA 90089-0802
213/740-5705
marketing@marshall.usc.edu
http://www.uscdma.org
Degrees available: Bachelor's degree

Southern Polytechnic State University
Department of Industrial Engineering Technology
1100 South Marietta Parkway, Building M, Room 108
Marietta, GA 30060
678/915-7243
http://iet.spsu.edu/IET_Program.html
Degrees available: Bachelor's degree

Texas A&M University
Department of Engineering Technology and Industrial Distribution
3367 TAMU
College Station, Texas 77843-3367
979/845-4984
http://id.tamu.edu
Degrees available: Bachelor's degree, master's degree (master's degree is an online program)

Did You Know?

Distribution of industrial products in the United States is a $4 trillion business—or more than 10 percent of the gross national product.

For More Information:

Industrial Supply Association
1300 Sumner Avenue
Cleveland, OH 44115-2851
866/460-2360
info@isapartners.org
http://www.ida-assoc.org/

National Association of Industrial Technology
3300 Washtenaw Avenue, Suite 220
Ann Arbor, MI 48104-4200
734/677-0720
nait@nait.org
http://www.nait.org

Integrated Marketing Communications

Blending coursework from its school of business and school of communications, Ithaca College's (new in 2004) integrated marketing communications degree teaches students how to examine the natural connections between what were once seen as separate disciplines— public relations, marketing, advertising, sales promotion, and electronic marketing. Attracting the attention of today's consumers—especially in a world of podcasts, cable television, the 24-hour newscycle, and the Internet—is increasingly difficult, yet key if businesses are to be successful. Students gain fun and practical experience developing and presenting communications strategies for real companies and work at such diverse internship placements as all four major American television networks, Capitol Records, Comedy Central, DDB Worldwide, and National Public Radio.

Typical Courses:

> Advertising
> Public Relations
> Marketing
> Consumer Behavior
> Research Methods
> Quantitative Mass Media Research Methods
> Media Writing
> Statistics
> Consumer Behavior
> Marketing on the Internet

Potential Employers:

> Advertising agencies
> Public relations firms
> Governmental agencies
> Nonprofit organizations
> Media outlets
> Corporations

Available At:

Ithaca College
Department of Television-Radio
Integrated Marketing Communications Program
953 Danby Road
Ithaca, NY 14850
607/274-3260
http://www.ithaca.edu
Degrees available: Bachelor's degree

For More Information:

Advertising Educational Foundation
220 East 42nd Street, Suite 3300
New York, NY 10017-5806
http://www.aded.org

American Advertising Federation
1101 Vermont Avenue, NW, Suite 500
Washington, DC 20005-6306
http://www.aaf.org

American Marketing Association
311 South Wacker Drive, Suite 5800
Chicago, IL 60606
http://www.marketingpower.com

Public Relations Society of America
33 Maiden Lane, 11th Floor
New York, NY 10038-5150
http://www.prsa.org

Did You Know?

Ithaca Ad Lab students recently developed a national communications strategy for Yahoo!; this award-winning campaign was later presented to Yahoo! and a panel of top advertising executives at the annual National Student Advertising Competition sponsored by the American Advertising Federation.

Internet Communications

New technologies are radically changing the way people and organizations use the Internet. The joining of Internet, telephone, and television technology with DSL, cable-modem, cellular and satellite technology creates a necessity for trained professionals in this rapidly emerging technological field. A major in Internet communications helps students gain the knowledge and skills needed to put them in the forefront of anticipating—and even shaping—the Internet revolution. Graduates work as writers, editors, information architects, content developers, publication managers, usability specialists, corporate curriculum designers and trainers, documentation specialists, proposal writers, and freelancers. For those who want a cutting edge advantage over the classic English major in an interdisciplinary, high-tech environment, this major might just be for you.

Typical Courses:

> Calculus
> Web Design and Management
> Technical Writing
> Data Structures and Algorithms
> Operating Systems
> Document Design
> Verbal and Visual Communication
> Linguistics

Potential Employers:

> Small and large businesses and corporations
> Publishing companies
> Internet companies
> Web design agencies

Did You Know?

Professional and technical communication is one of the 20 fastest growing fields in the United States, according to the federal government.

Available At:

Illinois Institute of Technology
3300 South Federal Street
Chicago, IL 60616-3793
admission@iit.edu
http://www.iit.edu/admission/undergrad/programs/icom/#careerop
Degrees available: Bachelor's degree

For More Information:

Information Technology Association of America
1401 Wilson Boulevard, Suite 1100
Arlington, VA 22209
703/522-5055
http://www.itaa.org

Online News Association
PO Box 30702
Bethesda, MD 20824
617/698-5252
http://www.onlinenewsassociation.org

Landmark College

Landmark College in Putney, Vermont, is one of two colleges in the United States that offers an educational program that is designed exclusively for students with dyslexia, attention deficit hyperactivity disorder (ADHD), or other specific learning disabilities (LDs). The College offers an associate of arts degree in general studies that prepares students to transfer to bachelor's degree programs at four-year colleges and universities. It also offers an associate of arts degree in business studies. Landmark students can participate in six intercollegiate sports, including basketball, baseball, soccer, softball, volleyball, and equestrian. Its Academic Resource Center has 30,000+ volumes, including an extensive LD/ADHD collection. Additionally, study abroad options are available in England, Ireland, Greece, India, Italy, and Spain.

Available Fields of Study:

> General Studies
> Business Studies

For More Information:

Landmark College
River Road South
Putney, VT 05346
802/387-6718
http://www.landmark.edu
Degrees available: Associate degree

Interview: Rob Bahny

The editors of *They Teach That in College!?* spoke with Rob Bahny, Associate Director of Admissions & Financial Aid at Landmark College, about his interesting college.

Q. Please briefly describe Landmark and the types of students it serves.

A. Landmark College is a small, residential, liberal arts college established in 1983 that offers associate degrees. Landmark exclusively serves students with ADHD and/or learning disabilities (dyslexia, disgraphia, reading disorder, disorder of written expression, etc.). We have 420 students and we are located in Putney, Vermont, which is a small town in the Connecticut River Valley in the southern part of the state. [By car], we are two hours from Boston, four hours from New York City, and three hours from Burlington, Vermont.

Q. What personal qualities should a student have to be successful at Landmark?

A. We are looking for students who are bright, mature, and motivated and who are interested in not only earning an associate degree, but who also have the desire to become more effective learners. A student coming to Landmark must be prepared to try many new things. Our professors are well versed in many different learning strategies, and they will ask students to try these strategies on a regular basis.

Q. What does your Learning Communities program offer students?

A. When students first start at Landmark, they are grouped with other students who are achieving at a similar academic level. This ensures that there is continuity in the curriculum and material that they are learning. Students will take classes with many of the same students in their community, so the program is also helpful in establishing peer groups.

Q. What types of four-year colleges do students transfer to after earning their associate degrees?

A. Students go to any number of schools after Landmark. Many of our students continue at small, liberal arts colleges, some go to Ivy League schools, and some have gone overseas to continue their education. Some of our more popular destinations include: University of Vermont, University of Denver, American University, Bentley College, Savannah College of Art and Design, College of Santa Fe, and Sarah Lawrence College. A complete list of these colleges is available at www.landmark.edu/admissions/power_of_degree.html#colleges.

Q. What summer opportunities are available at your school?

A. Landmark has three different summer programs. We have a three-week program for current high school students where they take classes in areas such as writing, study skills, communications, or math. There is a High School to College Transition program that is two weeks long and is intended to help close the gap between high school and college.

Also, we have a three-week College Skills program for current college students in addition to credit courses for current Landmark students. This is intended to help college students who are struggling. The program aims to improve their skills in areas such as writing, communications, project/time management, etc.

All of these programs are intended for proactive and motivated students who can acknowledge that they need to improve their academic skills so that they can become better students. Each program is organized to serve the distinct and unique educational needs of students at that particular stage of their educational career.

149

Q. What does the future hold for Landmark?

A. The future for Landmark continues to look very bright. As more and more people become aware of our college and the uniqueness of what we do through our stepped-up recruiting efforts, we see our enrollment continuing to grow. We are able to become more selective and admit a student body that will be able to gain the most from our associate degree programs. Our student body continues to become more diverse, and our students continue to bring many different and exciting talents to our campus community.

Landscape Design

If you've ever admired a well-designed and beautiful park, playground, garden, college or high school campus, country club, shopping center, zoo, or even skate park, then you've seen the work of a landscape architect firsthand. Landscape architects analyze, plan, design, and manage outdoor spaces. They use computer-aided design software, computer mapping systems, and other tools to design outdoor spaces that not only serve practical needs, but also protect the environment. You will need a bachelor's or master's degree in landscape architecture to work in this field. Employment prospects for landscape architects are excellent. The U.S. Department of Labor predicts that the career of landscape architect will grow faster than the average for all occupations through 2012. Approximately 30,000 landscape architects are employed in the United States, according to the American Society of Landscape Architects.

Typical Courses:

> Landscape Design Methods
> Plans and Design
> Landscape Graphics
> Regional Landscape History
> Landscape Construction
> The Urban Landscape
> World Gardens
> Landscape Architectural Practice
> Drawing the Landscape

Potential Employers:

> Consulting firms
> Public agencies
> Landscape construction and nursery companies
> National Park Service
> U.S. Forest Service
> Bureau of Land Management
> Other governmental agencies
> Self-employment

Available At:

This list of schools offering programs in landscape design is not exhaustive. For more accredited programs, visit http://www.asla.org.

Arizona State University
School of Architecture and Landscape Architecture
PO Box 871905
Tempe, AZ 85287-1905
caed.advising@asu.edu
Degrees available: Bachelor's degree

California State Polytechnic University
Department of Landscape Architecture
3801 West Temple Avenue
Pomona, CA 91768
http://www.csupomona.edu/~la
Degrees available: Bachelor's degree, master's degree

Colorado State University
Department of Horticulture and Landscape Architecture
111 Shepardson Building
Fort Collins, CO 80523-1173
http://www.colostate.edu/Depts/LArch
Degrees available: Bachelor's degree

University of Connecticut
Department of Plant Science
1376 Storrs Road, U-4067
Storrs, CT 06269-4067
http://www.canr.uconn.edu/plsci/la/index.html
Degrees available: Bachelor's degree

Did You Know?

Approximately 23 percent of landscape architects are self employed, according to the American Society of Landscape Architects. That's more than three times the average for workers in all occupations.

University of Florida
Department of Landscape Architecture
336 Architecture Building, PO Box 115704-5704
Gainesville, FL 32611
http://www.dcp.ufl.edu/landscape
Degrees available: Bachelor's degree, master's degree

University of Georgia
School of Environmental Design
609 Caldwell Hall
Athens, GA 30602-1845
http://www.sed.uga.edu
Degrees available: Bachelor's degree, master's degree

University of Idaho
Landscape Architecture Department
PO Box 442481
Moscow, ID 83844-2481
http://www.uidaho.edu/larch
Degrees available: Bachelor's degree

University of Illinois
Department of Landscape Architecture
611 Lorado Taft Drive, 101 Temple Hoyne Buell Hall
Champaign, IL 61820
217/333-0176
LADept@uiuc.edu
http://www.landarch.uiuc.edu
Degrees available: Bachelor's degree, master's degree

University of Kentucky
Department of Landscape Architecture
S305 Agriculture Science North
Lexington, KY 40546-0091
859/257-7295
http://www.uky.edu/Agriculture/LA
Degrees available: Bachelor's degree

Louisiana State University
School of Landscape Architecture
302 College of Design Building
Baton Rouge, LA 70803-7020
225/578-1434
laadm1@lsu.edu
http://www.design.lsu.edu
Degrees available: Bachelor's degree, master's degree

University of Maryland
Department of Natural Resource Sciences and Landscape Architecture
2139A Plant Sciences Building
College Park, MD 20742
mdosh@umd.edu
http://www.larch.umd.edu
Degrees available: Bachelor's degree

North Dakota State University
Department of Architecture and Landscape Architecture
PO Box 5285 S.U. Station
Fargo, ND 58105-5285
http://www.ndsu.edu/ndsu/landarch
Degrees available: Bachelor's degree

University of Oregon
Department of Landscape Architecture
5234 University of Oregon, 230 Lawrence Hall
Eugene, OR 97403-5234
landarch@uoregon.edu
http://landarch.uoregon.edu
Degrees available: Bachelor's degree, master's degree

Purdue University
Department of Horticulture and Landscape Architecture
625 Agriculture Mall Drive
West Lafayette, IN 47907-2010
http://www.hort.purdue.edu/hort/landarch/landarch.shtml
Degrees available: Bachelor's degree

Texas A&M University
Department of Landscape Architecture and Urban Planning
3137 TAMU
College Station, TX 77843-3137
http://archone.tamu.edu/LAUP
Degrees available: Bachelor's degree, master's degree

For More Information:

American Society of Landscape Architects
636 Eye Street, NW
Washington, DC 20001-3736
http://www.asla.org

LAprofession.org
http://www.laprofession.org

Medical Illustration

Are you a talented artist with a fascination for medicine, biology, and related fields? If so, you may have a career as a medical illustrator in your future. Medical illustrators, according to the Association of Medical Illustrators, are "professional artists . . . who create visual material to help record and disseminate medical, biological, and related knowledge." They illustrate medical and surgical procedures and techniques and biological and anatomical structures (such as the human heart, the bones of the foot, and arteries and veins) and processes. They may also create work in three dimensions, such as models for simulated medical procedures and anatomical teaching models. A master's degree in medical illustration is required for most positions in medical illustration. Four colleges in the United States and one in Canada offer accredited graduate programs in medical illustration (see below).

154

Typical Courses:

> Digital Illustration
> Reference Photography
> Two- and three-dimensional design
> Head, Hands, and Facial Expressions
> Figures in Motion
> General and Human Biology
> Human Gross Anatomy
> Zoological and Botanical Illustration
> 3-D Model Design
> Anatomical Visualization

Potential Employers:

> Hospitals
> Medical centers
> Specialty clinics
> Medical organizations
> Medical journals
> Colleges and universities
> Private companies
> Book and magazine publishers
> Advertising agencies

> Pharmaceutical and medical product companies
> Law firms

Available At:

University of Illinois-Chicago
College of Associated Health Professions
Department of Biomedical Visualization
1919 West Taylor Street, Room 213, M/C 527
Chicago, IL 60612
312/996-7337
http://www.ahs.uic.edu/bhis
Degrees available: Master's degree

Did You Know?

The Biomedical Visualization program at the University of Illinois-Chicago has the only comprehensive program in prosthetics/3-D model design in the world.

John Hopkins University
Department of Art as Applied to Medicine
1830 East Monument Street, Suite 7000
Baltimore, MD 21205-2100
410/955-3213
info@medart.jhu.edu
http://www.med.jhu.edu/medart
Degrees available: Master's degree

Medical College of Georgia
Department of Medical Illustration
1120 15th Street, CJ1101
Augusta, GA 30912-0300
706/721-3266
medart@mcg.edu
http://www.mcg.edu/medart
Degrees available: Master's degree

Rochester Institute of Technology
School of Art
One Lomb Memorial Drive
Rochester, NY 14623-5603
585/475-2411

http://www.rit.edu/~932www/ugrad_bulletin/colleges/cias/sart.html
Degrees available: Bachelor's degree

University of Texas
Department of Biomedical Communications
Southwestern Medical Center at Dallas
5323 Harry Hines Boulevard
Dallas, TX 75235-8881
214/648-4699
biocomm@utsouthwestern.edu
http://www.utsouthwestern.edu/biomedcom
Degrees available: Master's degree

University of Toronto
Department of Biomedical Communications
Institute of Medical Science
Medical Sciences Building, Room 2356
1 King's College Circle
Toronto, ON M5S 1A8 Canada
416/978-2659
http://www.bmc.med.utoronto.ca/bmc
Degrees available: Master's degree

156

For More Information:

Association of Medical Illustrators
810 East Tenth Street
Lawrence, KS 66044
hq@ami.org
http://medical-illustrators.org

BioCommunications Association, Inc.
220 Southwind Lane
Hillsborough, NC 27278
919/245-0906
office@bca.org
http://www.bca.org

Health and Science Communications Association
39 Wedgewood Drive, Suite A
Jewett City, CT 06351
860/376-5915
http://www.hesca.org

Interview: Steven Harrison

Steven Harrison is the Chairman of the Department of Medical Illustration at the Medical College of Georgia, which is located in Augusta, Georgia. He discussed his program and the education of medical illustration students with the editors of *They Teach That in College!?*

Q. Please provide an overview of your medical illustration program.

A. Medical illustrators are specially trained artists who communicate complex scientific ideas in a meaningful, aesthetic, and understandable manner. They create visuals for a variety of audiences and media, including art for print (textbooks, journals, magazines, and posters), and projection (animation and still art for television, classroom, and interactive multimedia presentations). Medical illustrators are employed in medical schools, urban medical centers, large hospitals, and specialty clinics. They may work in single-artist studios or large production departments. Advertising agencies, publishers, and pharmaceutical and medical product companies use the services of private-practice medical illustrators. Attorneys may commission medical illustrators to produce artwork to be used as demonstrative evidence in the courtroom.

157

The Medical Illustration Graduate Program at the Medical College of Georgia has been in existence since 1949 and offers a two-year (five semesters, 21 months) curriculum leading to a Master of Science degree in Medical Illustration. The curriculum combines coursework in the basic medical sciences (human gross anatomy, cell biology, histology, pathology), mostly taken with medical students, and instruction in illustration techniques in traditional and digital media. Problem solving assignments stress clarity and accuracy of scientific content and storytelling directed to specific audiences and education levels (professional, patient, and/or lay public). Students spend considerable time drawing from the human cadaver and other references, as well as observing and sketching in the operating room.

Admission to the program is competitive and based on academic performance, a portfolio of artwork demonstrating advanced drawing and painting ability, and a personal interview. A baccalaureate degree is required, as are prerequisite courses in human physiology and comparative vertebrate anatomy/morphology.

Q. What are the most important personal and professional qualities for medical illustration majors?

A. Medical illustration majors should have advanced drawing and painting skills, as demonstrated by a comprehensive portfolio of artwork. We prefer to see artwork that is drawn from life and not from photographic reference. Even though professional illustrators may use some photographic references, medical illustrators often draw what cannot be seen, and thus must have strong conceptualization abilities when direct reference materials are unavailable. Prospective students should also have a keen interest in science. The ability to conceptualize complex subject matter and reconstruct information into a visual story is most important. Creativity and problem solving skills are invaluable to any successful illustrator. It is important to be able to produce high quality work under tight deadline schedules.

Many prospective medical illustration students have undergraduate majors in art (usually drawing and painting). However, perhaps a third of our applicants major in the biological sciences with a minor in art. Realistic rendering skills and attention to detail are hallmarks of the profession.

Q. What advice would you offer MI majors as they graduate and look for jobs?

A. Job placement in the field of medical illustration is quite good for recent graduates. It may be necessary to relocate to different geographic locations to secure employment, so the graduating student must be flexible in this regard. A professional quality portfolio and resume are essential to gaining employment. Additional skills in digital media (e.g., animation and Web design), graphic design, and writing make the individual more valuable to an employer.

Q. What educational level is typically required for medical illustration graduates to land good jobs in the industry?

A. All medical illustration programs accredited by the Association of Medical Illustrators and the Commission on Accreditation of Allied Health Education Programs must be at the graduate (master's degree) level. Professional certification is available to graduates of accredited programs or individuals who have practiced in the field for five or more years. Certification examination and credentials are administered by the Board of Certification for Medical Illustrators.

Q. How will the field of medical illustration change in the future?

A. The future of the profession of medical illustration has been, and will continue to be, influenced by developing technologies in communication and computer graphics. Knowledge of these technologies and visual graphics software is becoming a necessity for the practicing illustrator, although strong drawing and conceptualization skills remain key. I am often asked if the computer is going to replace the medical illustrator. The computer is merely one of the many artistic tools with which we work, and new technologies have created an even greater need for the trained and knowledgeable medical illustrator. The growing mass of scientific and medical knowledge, and the increasing need to communicate such and educate more audiences, will provide a greater need for medical illustrators. For example, in the last few years, I have seen an increase in the use of, and jobs in, medical animation and 3-D modeling.

Motorsport Engineering

Are you a fan of auto racing? Do you like designing and building things? If so, the Motorsport Engineer Program at Colorado State University may help you put the pedal to the metal when it comes to preparing for a career in motorsport engineering. The graduate-level (master's and Ph.D.) program seeks to train motorsport engineers in vehicle design, vehicle setup, and race preparation. Graduates work as *motorsport design engineers,* who design and analyze competitive race vehicles, and *motorsport team engineers,* who work as a member of a race team to improve the competitiveness of the vehicle and driver. To be eligible for graduate programs, students must have a bachelor's degree in an engineering field. Program facilities include state-of-the-art computational facilities, testing areas, and laboratories.

Typical Courses:

> Vehicle Dynamics
> Computational Fluid Dynamics
> Internal Combustion Engines
> Advanced Mechanical Systems
> Experimental Methods and Measurements
> Advanced Mechanics of Materials
> Fundamentals of Vibrations
> Finite Element Method
> Mathematical Analysis
> Design and Data Analysis for Researchers

Potential Employers:

> Racing teams
> Automobile manufacturers

Did You Know?

Colorado State University Motorsport Engineering graduates are already key members of two Champ Car World Series teams.

Available At:

Colorado State University
College of Engineering
Fort Collins, CO 80523
970/491-6220
http://www.engr.colostate.edu/me/motorsport
Degrees available: Master's degree, doctorate degree

For More Information:

American Society for Engineering Education
1818 N Street, NW, Suite 600
Washington, DC 20036-2479
202/331-3500
http://www.asee.org

Junior Engineering Technical Society, Inc.
1420 King Street, Suite 405
Alexandria, VA 22314
703/548-5387
info@jets.org
http://www.jets.org

161

Society of Manufacturing Engineers
One SME Drive, PO Box 930
Dearborn, MI 48121
800/733-4763
http://www.sme.org

Music Business

The music business is much more than just the performers we hear on the radio and see in concert or in videos on TV. Who works behind the scenes to make the stars look good? Who engineers the recording of a hit song? Who promotes the band and its merchandise? Who books shows and plans entire concert tours? People with a love for music and a head for business work behind-the scenes in this demanding, yet rewarding, industry. They handle all of the tasks mentioned above and more. Several schools across the United States now offer degrees that address the business side of music, preparing students for careers as music executives, sales representatives, music producers, music distributors, talent managers, recording engineers, sound technicians, booking agents, concert venue managers, music retailers, and more. Degrees in music business and related fields are available at all academic levels.

Typical Courses:

> Music Theory
> Music History
> Music Merchandising
> Accounting
> Principal Instrument/Voice
> Artist Management
> Music Copyright and Publishing
> Marketing and Advertising
> Basic or Choral Conducting
> Record Industry Operations
> Consumer Behavior
> Arts Administration and Venue Management

Potential Employers:

> Artist management agencies
> Music distributors
> Music production companies
> Music promoters
> Music publishers
> Music retailers
> Postsecondary institutions

> Professional symphonies and opera companies
> Recording studios

Available At:

The following list of schools offering programs in music business is not exhaustive. For more programs, visit the Music and Entertainment Industry Educators Association's website, http://www.meiea.org.

Belmont University
Mike Curb College of Entertainment and Music Business
1900 Belmont Boulevard
Nashville, TN 37212
http://www.belmont.edu/mb
Degrees available: Bachelor's degree

Eastern Kentucky University
Department of Music
521 Lancaster Avenue, 101 Foster Building
Richmond, KY 40475-3102
http://www.music.eku.edu
Degrees available: Bachelor's degree

Houston College (multiple campuses)
http://www.hccs.edu/discipline/musb/musb.htm
Degrees available: Certificate, associate degree

Lewis University
Department of Music
One University Parkway
Romeoville, IL 60446
music@lewisu.edu
http://www2.lewisu.edu/%7Emcferrmi
Degrees available: Bachelor's degree

University of Massachusetts-Lowell
Department of Music
35 Wilder Street, Suite 3
Lowell, MA 01854-3083
http://www.uml.edu/College/arts_sciences/fineartsframe.htm
Degrees available: Bachelor's degree

University of Miami
Frost School of Music
Department of Music Media and Industry

PO Box 248165
Coral Gables, FL 33124-7610
http://www.music.miami.edu/programs/mbei/mbei.html
Degrees available: Bachelor's degree, master's degree

Miami Dade Community College (multiple campuses)
305/237-8888
mdccinfo@mdc.edu
https://sisvsr.mdc.edu/ps/sheet.aspx
Degrees available: Associate degree

University of Southern California
Department of Music Industry
Los Angeles, CA 90089
http://www.usc.edu/music/academic/programs/industry.html
Degrees available: Bachelor's degree

Valparaiso University
Department of Arts and Sciences
Valparaiso, IN 46383-6493
http://www.valpo.edu/music/BAMusIndustry.html
Degrees available: Bachelor's degree

164

University of Wisconsin-Oshkosh
800 Algoma Boulevard
Oshkosh WI 54901
music@uwosh.edu
http://www.uwosh.edu/departments/music/degree/musicindust.html
Degrees available: Bachelor's degree

For More Information:

American Marketing Association
311 South Wacker Drive, Suite 5800
Chicago, IL 60606
800/262-1150
info@ama.org
http://www.marketingpower.com

American Society of Composers, Authors, and Publishers
One Lincoln Plaza
New York, NY 10023
212/621-6000
http://www.ascap.org

National Association of Schools of Music
11250 Roger Bacon Drive, Suite 21

Reston, VA 20190-5248
703/437-0700
info@arts-accredit.org
http://nasm.arts-accredit.org

Recording Industry Association of America
1330 Connecticut Avenue, NW, Suite 300
Washington, DC 20036
202/775-0101
http://www.riaa.com

Interview: Marcia Lewis

Valparaiso University in Valparaiso, Indiana, offers an interdisciplinary program in music and business that leads to a Bachelor of Arts degree in Music (Music Industry Option). The editors of *They Teach That in College!?* discussed this interesting program with Professor Marcia Lewis, Associate Professor of Music.

Q. Please tell us about your program.

A. Music Enterprises is an innovative, four-year interdisciplinary program in music and business designed to prepare students for management positions in arts administration and the manufacturing, publishing, distribution, and retailing aspects of the music industry. Students take 40 credits of music, including three specialized music business courses (survey, legal aspects, and current issues) as well as an internship. The 31-credit business minor includes courses in math, accounting, economics, business law, statistics, management, marketing, and finance.

Q. What high school subjects/activities should students focus on to be successful in this major?

A. I think students need a solid background in mathematics and computer technology. They also need to take speech and writing courses. Economics is also beneficial to this major. Their activities should include work in management and production, if possible.

Q. What are the most important personal and professional qualities for music merchandising majors?

A. Individuals in this major need to have an outgoing personality, good writing and verbal skills, entrepreneurial and organizational abilities, and be creative people with a passion for music.

Q. What advice would you offer music merchandising majors as they graduate and look for jobs?

A. Be persistent and realistic in your search for an entry-level position into the music industry. Your ultimate goal may be to be a producer, but this is not where you start. You have to network and go to trade shows and conferences to get into the industry. You must be aggressive in your search for a job.

Q. What educational level is typically required for music merchandising graduates to land good jobs in the industry?

A. A bachelor's degree is most common to land your first job. A master's degree (probably in business) may be required to advance professionally. This is presently the terminal degree in the music industry.

Q. Where do music merchandising graduates find employment?

A. Entry-level jobs are available in the music products fields and arts administration. It's presently very difficult to find entry-level jobs in the recording industry because this sector of the industry is laying off rather than hiring personnel.

Q. How will the field of music merchandising change in the future?

A. The field of music merchandising will continue to become more entrepreneurship- and technology-based in the future. Changes in the industry have always been fast-paced, but presently the business model is completely changing and charging forward at a rather overwhelming pace. The future is wide open.

Music Theatre Writing

Students who enjoy writing for musical theatre and opera may be interested in learning more about the Graduate Musical Theatre Writing Program at New York University. What are the major criteria for admission to this program? According to the Program's website, "talent, originality, and an ability to work well in collaboration." Students in the program participate in writing workshops that help them develop their creative voice, collaborate with others, and learn about genres and storytelling techniques. They also attend integrated craft and history seminars, which provide an overview of music in theatre through the years, as well as participate in fieldwork opportunities in New York City, the capital of the U.S. theatre industry. Students complete the program by writing a full-length theatrical work.

Typical Courses:

> Musical Theater Structures
> Joint Playwriting Tutorial
> Seminar: Critique
> Musical Theater History
> Tutorials, Seminars, and Labs (on various topics)
> Creative Producing
> Seminar: Collaboration

Potential Employers:

> Theatrical production companies

Did You Know?

Accomplished alumni of NYU's Graduate Musical Theatre Writing program include Winnie Holzman (class of 1981), bookwriter of the Broadway hit *Wicked;* David Javerbaum (class of 1995), Emmy Award-winning head writer of *The Daily Show* with Jon Stewart and lyricist for the Broadway musical version of John Waters' film, *Cry-Baby;* and Mindi Dickstein (class of 1993), lyricist for the Broadway musical version of *Little Women.*

Available At:

New York University
Graduate Musical Theatre Writing Program Office
113-A Second Avenue
New York, NY 10003
212/998-1830
musical.theatre@nyu.edu
http://gmtw.tisch.nyu.edu/page/home
Degrees available: Master's degree

For More Information:

National Association of Schools of Theater
11250 Roger Bacon Drive, Suite 21
Reston, VA 20190-5248
703/437-0700
info@arts-accredit.org
http://www.arts-accredit.org

168

Theater Communications Group
520 Eighth Avenue, 24th Floor
New York, NY 10018-4156
212/609-5900
tcg@tcg.org
http://www.tcg.org

Music Therapy

Although music has been used informally for centuries to achieve therapeutic goals, it was not until World War I, when professional and amateur musicians visited veteran's hospitals to play music for injured veterans, that the medical community realized the healing power of music and began to incorporate this philosophy into health care regimens. Music therapy involves the use of music to accomplish a variety of therapeutic aims, including the restoration, maintenance, and improvement of mental and physical health. A music therapist may work with individuals of all ages who require treatment due to behavioral, social, learning, or physical disabilities. In essence, music is used as a tool to help people maintain or improve upon important life skills. Music therapy can be a satisfying career for individuals with strong musical backgrounds who are also interested in a health care profession. A bachelor's degree in music therapy is required to become a music therapist.

Typical Courses:

> Sociology
> Abnormal Psychology
> Music in Recreation
> Piano
> Percussion Methods
> Guitar Methods
> Studio Instruction
> Music Theory
> Music and Culture
> Music Therapy Techniques

Potential Employers:

> Hospitals
> Schools
> Rehabilitation centers
> Nursing homes
> Health care facilities

Available At:

More than 70 degree programs in 30 states, the District of Columbia, and Canada are approved by the American Music Therapy Association. For a complete list of schools, visit the following website, http://www.musictherapy.org/handbook/schools.html.

Arizona State University
School of Music
PO Box 870405
Tempe, AZ 85287-0405
480/965-3371
http://music.asu.edu/academics/bach_musictherapy.htm
Degrees available: Bachelor's degree

California State University-Northridge
18111 Nordhoff Street
Northridge, CA 91330-8314
818/677-3174
http://www.csun.edu/~hcmus006/MusicTherapy.html
Degrees available: Bachelor's degree

University of Georgia
School of Music
250 River Road
Athens, GA 30602-3153
706/542-2801
http://www.music.uga.edu/degree_programs/undergrad/
#BM-Therapy
Degrees available: Bachelor's degree, master's degree

Illinois State University
College of Fine Arts
Music Therapy Program
5660 School of Music
Normal, IL 61790-5660
309/438-8198
http://www.cfa.ilstu.edu/music/undergraduate/music_therapy.shtml
Degrees available: Bachelor's degree, master's degree

University of Iowa
School of Music
2040 Voxman Music Building
Iowa City, IA 52242
319/335-1657

http://www.uiowa.edu/~music/current/therapy_undergrad.htm
Degrees available: Bachelor's degree, master's degree

University of Miami
Frost School of Music
PO Box 248165
Coral Gables, FL 33124
305/284-3943
http://www.music.miami.edu/programs/med/med.html
Degrees available: Bachelor's degree, master's degree

University of Missouri-Kansas City
Conservatory of Music
4949 Cherry, 316 Grant Hall
Kansas City, MO 64110-2229
816/235-2920
http://conservatory.umkc.edu/musiceducationtherapy.asp
Degrees available: Bachelor's degree, master's degree, doctorate
degree

Temple University
Esther Boyer College of Music
Music Therapy Program
Philadelphia, PA 19122
215/204-8301
http://www.temple.edu/bulletin/Academic_programs/
schools_colleges/boyer/music/programs/music_thearapy/
music_therapy.shtm
Degrees available: Bachelor's degree, master's degree, doctorate
degree

West Texas A&M University
Department of Music & Dance
Canyon, TX 79016-0001
806/651-2822
http://www.wtamu.edu/academic/fah/mus/prospective/bmmt.html
Degrees available: Bachelor's degree

University of Wisconsin-Eau Claire
Department of Allied Health Professions
Haas 146
Eau Claire, WI 54702-4004
715/836-4260
http://www.uwec.edu/ph/mt
Degrees available: Bachelor's degree

For More Information:

American Music Therapy Association
8455 Colesville Road, Suite 1000
Silver Spring, MD 20910
301/589-3300
school@musictherapy.org
http://www.musictherapy.org

Interview: Barbara J. Crowe

Arizona State University (ASU) in Tempe, Arizona, is one of more than 70 U.S. and Canadian colleges and universities that offer American Music Therapy Association (AMTA)-approved music therapy programs. The editors of *They Teach That in College!?* spoke with Barbara J. Crowe, Director of the Music Therapy Program at ASU, about this growing field.

Q. What is music therapy?

A. Music therapy is a mental health/special education profession that uses music and the active engagement in music activities to help a client achieve non-musical, therapeutic goals.

Q. Please describe your program.

A. As with all music therapy degrees, music therapy is a music major, so students take private lessons on their instrument or voice area, play or sing in ensembles like orchestra or choir, take music theory and music history classes, and participate in other music skill-developing courses and experiences. They also take general-studies classes to fulfill graduation requirements with an emphasis on psychology and special education classes. Over the course of the four-year degree program, they take 22 hours in specific courses in music therapy, which includes four separate practical experiences working with a variety of clients in music therapy. They usually work one hour per week with their client or client group.

Q. What types of skills and interests do students who enter your program need to possess?

A. They must have an extensive musical background, have taken private lessons on their instrument or voice area, have participated in music groups and ensembles, and read music-both treble and bass clef at least.

Q. What do students do in your clinical internship program?

A. The internship is a six-month, full-time working experience in music therapy under the supervision of a board-certified music therapist working in that facility. The students do all the job responsibilities of a professional music therapist-they assess client needs and set goals and objectives, create and implement the music therapy session, attend staff meetings, order equipment, and write progress notes and other forms of documentation. The specific music therapy activity interventions used will depend on the type of disability the client has, his or her age, and the goals to be achieved.

173

Did You Know?

According to the American Music Therapy Association, music therapy can help children and adults who have developmental and learning disabilities, mental health needs, Alzheimer's disease and other aging-related conditions, brain injuries, physical disabilities, substance abuse problems, and acute and chronic pain.

Q. How does your on-campus Music Therapy Clinic prepare students for the career?

A. The ASU Music Therapy Clinic is one of the places where the students do their classes in practical experience. In this facility they usually work one-on-one with a child who has some form of disability. We tend to have children with autism, cognitive impairment, and developmental delay. These practical, working experiences are essential for the students to develop their skills in music therapy and to prepare them for their internship.

Q. What career paths are available to students who complete your program?

A. Once they complete the degree-including the six-month internship-they are eligible to take the certification exam for music therapists. If they pass this exam, they become music therapists-board certified and are eligible to take a music therapy job anywhere in the country. Music therapists work in special education programs in school systems, in general medical hospitals, in nursing homes and elder care centers, in drug and alcohol rehabilitation programs, in head injury and stroke rehabilitation hospitals, in group homes for the mentally handicapped, and in psychiatric hospitals and day-care programs.

Q. What is the future for your program and music therapy?

A. We'll be establishing a master's program in music therapy shortly, which will help music therapists develop their skills. There is increasing demand for music therapists, though this varies from place to place throughout the country. ASU will be establishing a new medical center, and we have plans to incorporate research projects and collaborative programs in this new center.

Musical Instrument Repair

Behind every top-performing professional symphony orchestra, high school band, and amateur musician lies the integral work of the music instrument repair technician. Although the musical instrument repair industry is small—nearly 5,000 U.S. workers in 2005—employment prospects are good for aspiring repairers willing to receive training via an apprenticeship or a formal music instrument repair program. Only five postsecondary institutions in the United States and Canada offer training in music instrument repair.

Typical Courses:

> Introduction to Music
> Introduction to Band Instrument Repair
> Shop Practices and Safety for Band Instrument Repair
> Dent Removal Techniques
> Soldering and Brazing Techniques
> Brass Techniques
> Woodwind Techniques
> The Percussion Instruments
> Mathematics for Band Instrument Repair
> Human Relations for Band Instrument Repair

Potential Employers:

> Musical instrument repair shops
> Manufacturers
> Colleges and universities

Available At:

Badger State Repair School
204 West Centralia Street
Elkhorn, WI 53121
262/723-4062
badgerschool@napbirt.org
Degrees available: None (the School offers a 48-week course in brass and woodwind instrument repair)

Keyano College
8115 Franklin Avenue
Fort McMurray, AB T9H 2H7 Canada

780/791-8979
mir@keyano.ca
http://www.keyano.ca/prospective_students/programs/
certificate_diploma/music_instrument_repair.htm
Degrees available: Associate degree

Minnesota State College-SE Technical
308 Pioneer Road
Red Wing, MN 55066
877/853-8324
http://www.southeastmn.edu/Programs/BandInstrumentRepair/
index.asp?rw=1&w=0&online=0&programID=9 (Band
Instrument Repair)
http://www.southeastmn.edu/Programs/MusicalStringInstrument
Repair/index.asp?rw=1&w=0&online=0&programID=10
(Musical String Instrument Repair and Building)
Degrees available: Certificate

Renton Technical College
3000 NE 4th Street
Renton, WA 98056
425/235-2352
http://www.rtc.edu/Programs/TrainingPrograms/BIRT
Degrees available: Certificate, associate degree

Western Iowa Tech Community College
4647 Stone Avenue
Sioux City, IA 51106
800/352-4649
http://www.witcc.cc.ia.us/programs/classes.cfm?id=45
Degrees available: Associate degree

For More Information:

Guild of American Luthiers
8222 South Park Avenue
Tacoma, WA 98408-5226
253/472-7853
http://www.luth.org

**National Association of Professional Band Instrument
Repair Technicians**
2026 Eagle Road, PO Box 51
Normal, IL 61761
309/452-4257
napbirt@napbirt.org
http://www.napbirt.org

Piano Technicians Guild
ptg@ptg.org
http://www.ptg.org

Interview: Rod Siljenberg

Western Iowa Tech Community College in Sioux City, Iowa, is one of only five schools in the United States and Canada that offer training in musical instrument repair. Rod Siljenberg has been an instructor in the Band Instrument Repair Technology program at the College for more than 15 years. He was kind enough to speak with the editors of *They Teach That in College!?* about his program.

Q. Please describe the band instrument repair program.

A. Our program, which was created 35 years ago, focuses on the repair of woodwind and brass band instruments. Students who complete the two-year program earn an Associate Degree of Applied Science. Our students come from all over the United States. Fifteen to 20 international students have participated in the program over the years. Our average class size is approximately 20 students.

177

Q. How do students in the program learn instrument repair?

A. Students learn music instrument repair via instructional classes, or lab time, where they work and restore instruments provided by local music repair shops. Instructional classes make up at least 60 percent of class time. Music dealers have been very supportive of our school. They send many instruments for our students to work on.

Q. How has the program changed over the years?

A. Today, the program is handled more as an academic offering than a trade option. Thirty years ago, female enrollment was probably 5 percent. Today, it's almost 50 percent. Additionally, our students are getting younger. A lot more are coming straight from high school.

Q. How do the expectations of high school students differ from those other types of students in your program?

A. This type of study is a little more involved than many recent high school graduates envision. They have to know a lot more things than they expected, such as metal alloys, manufacturing techniques, and other skills. The younger the student, the more surprised they are when it comes to the first batch of tests. As they go along in the program, they see the expectations of our staff and improve their performance.

Q. In addition to high school students, what other types of people enter your program?

A. We get a good number of mid-career changers. We also have many students who are studying music education or music performance, but decide in their last years of school that teaching is not for them or that they need to subsidize their musician careers with a secondary career. We find that these types of students are a little more in tune with educational expectations.

Q. What personal qualities should a student have to be successful in your program?

A. Successful students need patience, problem-solving skills, attention to detail, and a sense of craftmanship and pride. They also need mechanical ability, but this can be developed. Although it is a lot easier for students to be successful in the program if they have mechanical sense, we have also had successful students who entered the program with strong musical aptitude but little mechanical ability.

Q. What advice would you give students as they complete their degrees and look for jobs?

A. We consider our graduates to be advanced apprentices and try to equip them with strong fundamental skills that they can use to enter the workforce. I recommend that graduates take a position at a music shop that has at least two or three repair technicians with considerable experience. Working eight-hour days with these workers will help new graduates build on the instruction they received in school. The repetitive practice of working on instruments will allow them to get faster and better, therefore increasing their earning potential.

Q. Are college settings becoming a more popular training avenue for students interested in the field?

A. Yes. A school with a proven curriculum is the way to go, as apprenticeships are rare and the training is usually on an as-needed basis. Shops are too busy and don't have time to work with beginners.

Q. What is the future for the music instrument repair industry?

A. The industry is as good as it ever was or better. With Internet business increasing, the number of small music stores will decrease. I believe more repair technicians will be independent, doing repair for one or more dealers as well as the public.

National Technical Institute for the Deaf

Deaf and hard-of-hearing students face many unique challenges as they pursue higher education. To help these students prepare for rewarding careers, Congress established the National Technical Institute for the Deaf (NTID) in 1965. In 1968, the NTID became one of the Rochester Institute of Technology's colleges. Today, 1,100 deaf and hard-of-hearing students attend the Institute. The NTID offers more than 100 campus organizations and activities and dozens of men's and women's varsity, intramural, and club sports.

Available Fields of Study:

Students at the NTID can pursue associate degrees in more than 30 accredited programs and bachelor's and master's degrees in more than 200 programs offered by the Rochester Institute of Technology. In addition, hearing students can pursue associate and bachelor's degrees in American Sign Language-English Interpretations, and deaf and hearing students can pursue master's degrees in Secondary Education of Students who are Deaf or Hard of Hearing. Visit http://www.ntid.rit.edu/prospective/majors.php for more information.

For More Information:

National Technical Institute for the Deaf
Rochester Institute of Technology
52 Lomb Memorial Drive
Rochester, NY 14623
585/475-6700 (Voice/TTY)
http://www.ntid.rit.edu/index_flash.php
Degrees available: Associate degree, bachelor's degree, master's degree

Interview: T. Alan Hurwitz

Dr. T. Alan Hurwitz, Vice President, Rochester Institute of Technology and CEO/Dean, National Technical Institute for the Deaf, was kind enough to talk to the editors of *They Teach That in College!?* about the school and its programs.

Q. Please describe the Institute for our readers.

A. The National Technical Institute for the Deaf, part of Rochester Institute of Technology, provides deaf and hard-of-hearing students with outstanding state-of-the-art technical and professional education programs, complemented by a strong arts and sciences curriculum, that prepares them to live and work in the mainstream of a rapidly changing global community and enhances their lifelong learning. NTID is the recognized world leader in applied research designed to enhance the social, economic, and educational accommodation of deaf and hard-of-hearing people.

Q. What type of services and facilities are available for deaf and hard-of-hearing students at the NTID?

A. Deaf and hard-of-hearing students enjoy a wide array of services including access to interpreters, speech-to-text transcription, note takers, and tutors, as well as other communication strategies. Onsite audiologists provide services related to hearing and hearing aids, assistive devices, and cochlear implants; speech-language pathologists offer a broad range of speech and language services as well.

181

Dorms and classrooms are fully networked with state-of-the-art computers and multimedia technologies. Students enjoy more than 100 clubs, creative arts programs, student government and religious activities, and sports programs. RIT Campus Safety employs officers who are deaf and also trains hearing officers in various communication strategies.

Q. Does the NTID offer any cooperative educational opportunities or internships?

A. At NTID/RIT, we do offer cooperative educational opportunities and internships. In fact, in most cases, we require it. Employment specialists within the NTID Center on Employment work closely with students throughout their college years to help prepare them for successful, real-world employment. The co-op experience is a critical component of that. The employers-large and small companies throughout the United States-who hire our students for co-op frequently hire the students for permanent jobs. We're proud of our 93 percent employment placement rate at NTID, and we credit that to-in addition to their skills matching to the employers' needs-the fact that we work closely with the student and the employer in the beginning to overcome any challenges that may exist, such as communication. Employers repeatedly tell us how NTID students bring a different kind of preparedness to the job and how they approach challenges with a can-do attitude.

Q. Can you provide a brief overview of your Explore Your Future program for high school juniors?

A. We understand how difficult it is to decide what you want to do the rest of your life, so at our widely popular Explore Your Future week-long summer program, we give high school juniors an opportunity to gain some hands-on experience with a variety of jobs and careers. The students leave with a written summary of experiences and the results of career-interest testing. They meet deaf and hard-of-hearing students from all over the country and participate in sports, dances, multicultural dinners, captioned movies, and more.

Q. What does the future hold for the NTID?

A. We recently announced a new plan that reflects a very bright future for our students! Over the next few years, we will be making exciting changes to our academic programs, access services, and outreach efforts to even more closely align with our students' unique needs. As hearing aid technology continues to improve, and the use of cochlear implants increases, students are using their hearing more than they ever have in the past, which changes their needs for support. In addition, educators and employers around the world have looked to the NTID as a model for technical education programs for deaf and hard-of-hearing students. The knowledge we've acquired from our years of extensive research and experience is unprecedented, and we will be establishing a formal outreach consortium to share information more widely.

Naval Engineering/ Ocean Engineering

Ever wonder who developed the technology that discovered and explored the deep sea wreckage of the *Titanic,* as seen in the 1997 film of the same name? Or who is called on for expertise when a submarine is in trouble, in need of a rescue mission? Developing the technology used in such instances is the job of the *ocean engineer.* This fascinating field not only focuses on this undersea technology, but also any engineering applications that deal with the effects of the ocean on ships of all sizes at the surface level. And like any field relying on modern technology to advance its mission, ocean engineers are constantly adapting modern technological innovations to create and design systems that can further the advancement of the ocean engineering field. Students in most programs will be exposed to current research studies, whether it be in classroom study or in practical internships. Students considering a career in ocean or naval engineering should have a strong aptitude for math and science as well as an inquisitive nature and a desire to work with cutting-edge technological industry. Degrees in naval/ocean engineering are available at the baccalaureate, master's, and doctoral levels.

Typical Courses:

> Marine Hydrodynamics
> Marine Engineering
> Foundations of Ship Design
> Thermodynamics
> Physics and Chemistry
> Fluid Dynamics
> Marine Systems Manufacturing
> Marine Systems Production Strategy and Operations Management
> Environmental Ocean Dynamics
> Principles of Ocean Systems Engineering

Potential Employers:

> Governmental agencies
> Defense contractors

> Private industry
> Consulting firms
> U.S. Navy

Available At:

The following list of schools offering programs in naval and ocean engineering is not exhaustive. For a complete list of programs, visit http://www.sname.org/outreach_degree.htm or http://www.abet.org/accrediteac.asp.

California Maritime Academy
200 Maritime Academy Drive
Vallejo, CA 94590
707/654-1000
http://www.csum.edu/Academics/Majors/MET
Degrees available: Bachelor's degree

Florida Atlantic University
Department of Ocean Engineering
Boca Raton Campus
777 Glades Road
Boca Raton, FL 33431
561/297-3430
http://www.oe.fau.edu
Degrees available: Bachelor's degree, master's degree, doctorate degree

Florida Atlantic University
SeaTech Campus
101 North Beach Road
Dania Beach, Florida 33004
http://www.oe.fau.edu
Degrees available: Bachelor's degree, master's degree, doctorate degree

Florida Institute of Technology
Department of Marine and Environmental Systems
150 West University Boulevard
Melbourne, FL 32901
dmes@marine.fit.edu
http://www.fit.edu/AcadRes/dmes/ocean.html
Degrees available: Bachelor's degree, master's degree, doctorate degree

Massachusetts Institute of Technology
Department of Mechanical Engineering
77 Massachusetts Avenue, Room 3-173
Cambridge, MA 02139
617/253-4330
discoveroe@mit.edu
http://oe.mit.edu/discover
Degrees available: Master's degree

University of Michigan
Department of Naval Architecture and Marine Engineering
NA&ME Building
2600 Draper Road
Ann Arbor, MI 48109-2145
734/764-6470
name-info@umich.edu
http://www.engin.umich.edu/dept/name/name.html
Degrees available: Bachelor's degree, master's degree, doctorate degree

University of Rhode Island
Narragansett Bay Campus
Department of Ocean Engineering
217 Sheets Building
Narragansett, RI 02882
401/874-6139
http://www.oce.uri.edu
Degrees available: Bachelor's degree, master's degree, doctorate degree

Stevens Institute of Technology
Department of Civil, Environmental, and Ocean Engineering
Castle Point on Hudson
Hoboken, NJ 07030
http://www.stevens.edu/engineering/ceoe
Degrees available: Bachelor's degree, master's degree, doctorate degree

Texas A&M University
Department of Civil Engineering
c/o Head, Ocean Engineering Program
3136 TAMU
College Station, TX 77843-3136
http://oceaneng.civil.tamu.edu
Degrees available: Bachelor's degree, master's degree, doctorate degree

U.S. Naval Academy
Department of Naval Architecture and Ocean Engineering
Mail Stop 11d
590 Holloway Road
Annapolis, MD 21402-5042
410/293-6420
naoeweb@usna.edu
http://www.usna.edu/NAOE/index.html
Degrees available: Bachelor's degree

Virginia Tech University
Department of Aerospace and Ocean Engineering
215 Randolph Hall
Blacksburg, VA 24061
540/231-6611
http://www.aoe.vt.edu
Degrees available: Bachelor's degree, master's degree, doctorate degree

186 For More Information:

American Society for Engineering Education
1818 N Street, NW, Suite 600
Washington, DC 20036-2479
202/331-3500
http://www.asee.org

American Society of Naval Engineers
1452 Duke Street
Alexandria, VA 22314-3458
703/836-6727
http://www.navalengineers.org

Junior Engineering Technical Society, Inc.
1420 King Street, Suite 405
Alexandria, VA 22314
703/548-5387
info@jets.org
http://www.jets.org

Outdoor Education

Calling all nature lovers! Imagine this normal workday: guiding a white water trip through a Class V river run, teaching backpacking safety to a group of first-time campers, or marking a new path for backcountry skiing. A major in outdoor education will prepare you for these tasks and much more—and a career in one of the fastest growing segments of the recreation industry. Programs, whether a two-year associate degree, or traditional four-year bachelor's degree, are based on a theoretical foundation, as well as practical experience ranging from kayaking to avalanche awareness. Most programs focus on the adventure or the environmental aspects interdependently, but students should look into each program in depth to discover programs that focus on one more than another, according to their interests. Programs emphasize outdoor program administration, team building, problem solving, adventure leadership, and natural resource management. Degrees in outdoor education are available at the two- and four-year level.

Typical Courses:

> Organization and Management of Adventure Programs
> Environmental Health and Safety
> Mountaineering
> Ecotourism and Natural Resource Management
> Scuba Diving
> Wilderness Survival and First Aid
> Marine Survival
> Fly Fishing
> Backpacking
> Cross Country Skiing
> Sociology of Sport

Potential Employers:

> National Park Service
> National Forest Service
> State and local parks and recreation agencies
> Outward Bound
> College/university outdoor programs
> Adventure-based residential treatment programs for at-risk youth

Available At:

Black Hills State University
1200 University Street, Unit 9502
Spearfish, SD 57799-9502
800/ALL-BHSU
http://www.bhsu.edu/academics/index.html
Degrees available: Bachelor's degree

Feather River College
Outdoor Recreation Leadership Program
570 Golden Eagle Avenue
Quincy, CA 95971
530/283-0202, ext. 275, 800/442-9799, ext. 275
http://www.frc.edu/ORL/contact.htm
Degrees available: Associate degree

Georgia College and State University
Department of Kinesiology
Coordinator of Outdoor Education Academic Programs
Campus Box 65
Milledgeville, GA 31061
478/445-4072
http://www.gcsu.edu/acad_affairs/school_healthsci/
HPER/BSOutdoorEd.htm
Degrees available: Bachelor's degree

Did You Know?

Outdoor adventure leadership students often have the opportunity to pursue more advanced travel and ecotourism adventures in areas such as Mexico's Baja peninsula and the south island of New Zealand.

Ithaca College
Department of Therapeutic Recreation and Leisure Services
953 Danby Road
Ithaca, NY 14850
607/274-3335
http://departments.ithaca.edu/trls/directory
Degrees available: Bachelor's degree

Malone College
School of Education
Department of Health and Human Performance
515 25th Street, NW
Canton, OH 44709
330/471-8590
http://www.malone.edu/2183
Degrees available: Bachelor's degree

University of Minnesota-Duluth
College of Education and Human Service Professions
Recreation Outdoor Education Program
120 Bohannon Hall, 1207 Ordean Court
Duluth, MN 55812
218/726-7442
cehsp@d.umn.edu
http://www.d.umn.edu/catalogs/current/umd/colleges/29.html
Degrees available: Bachelor's degree

Sheldon Jackson College
Outdoor Leadership Department
801 Lincoln Street
Sitka, AK 99835
800/478-4556
mkaplan@sj-alaska.edu
http://www.sheldonjackson.edu/519.cfm
Degrees available: Bachelor's degree

189

For More Information:

Outdoor Industry Association
4909 Pearl East Circle, Suite 200
Boulder, CO 80301
303/444-3353
info@outdoorindustry.org
http://www.outdoorindustry.org

Packaging Science

Nearly every product we purchase comes in some sort of packaging. And every package has to serve one or more purposes—it must keep the product adequately protected and/or fresh and it must be pleasing to the eye of the consumer. The packaging scientist must have an aptitude for both science and technology, a keen eye for design, and creative marketing business sensibility. This $100+ billion-a-year industry continues to grow in a society that purchases more than 500 billion packages annually in the United States alone, and there are currently only a handful of college programs helping to fill the increasing demand for graduates in this field. Degrees in packaging science are available at all academic levels.

Typical Courses:

> Principles of Packaging
> Consumer Products Packaging
> Packaging, Society and Environment
> Food Packaging
> Computer Tools for Packaging
> Distribution and Transport Packaging
> Packaging Production and Processing
> Package Decoration
> Analytical Methods in Packaging
> Senior Design in Packaging

Potential Employers:

> Packaging material manufacturers
> Converters (e.g., Sealed Air, Mitsubishi, Sonoco, International Paper, Georgia-Pacific, Smurfit, etc.)
> Packaging users (major food and medical companies)
> Parcel service and government organizations

Available At:

This list of schools offering programs in packaging science is not exhaustive. For more programs, visit the following website: http://users.erols.com/niphle/Schools.html.

Christian Brothers University
School of Engineering
650 East Parkway South
Memphis, TN 38104
901/321-3418
http://www.cbu.edu/engineering/packaging
Degrees available: Certificate

Clemson University
Department of Packaging Science
B-212 Poole Agricultural Center
Clemson, SC 29634
864/656-7637
http://www.clemson.edu/packaging
Degrees available: Bachelor's degree, master's degree

University of Florida
College of Agricultural and Life Sciences
PO Box 110570
Gainesville, FL 32611
352/392-1864, ext. 111
http://www.agen.ufl.edu/newsite/undergraduatepages/packaging/undergraduatepackagingindex.htm
Degrees available: Bachelor's degree

Indiana State University
Department of Industrial and Mechanical Technology
John T. Myers Technology Center
Terre Haute, IN 47809
812/237-3352
http://www.indstate.edu/imt
Degrees available: Bachelor's degree

Michigan State University
School of Packaging
East Lansing, MI 48824-1223
517/355-9580
package@packaging.msu.edu
http://packaging.msu.edu
Degrees available: Bachelor's degree, master's degree, doctorate degree

Rochester Institute of Technology
One Lomb Memorial Drive
Rochester, NY 14623-5603
585/475-2411

http://www.rit.edu/~703www
Degrees available: Bachelor's degree, master's degree

San Jose State University
Department of Industrial and Systems Engineering
Packaging Program
One Washington Square, Room 485B
San Jose, CA 95192
408/924-7851
http://www.engr.sjsu.edu/ise/pkg
Degrees available: Bachelor's degree

University of Wisconsin-Stout
College of Technology, Engineering, and Management
281F Technology Wing, Jarvis Hall
Menomonie, WI 54751-0790
715/232-1246
neuburgk@uwstout.edu
http://www.uwstout.edu/programs/bsp
Degrees available: Bachelor's degree

For More Information:

Institute of Packaging Professionals
1601 North Bond Street, Suite 101
Naperville, IL 60563
630/544-5050
info@iopp.org
http://www.iopp.org

National Institute of Packaging Handling and Logistics Engineers
6902 Lyle Street
Lanham, MD 20706-3454
301/459-9105
niphle@erols.com
http://users.erols.com/niphle

Packaging Machinery Manufacturers Institute
4350 North Fairfax Drive, Suite 600
Arlington, VA 22203
888/275-7664
pmmiwebhelp@PMMI.org
http://www.pmmi.org

Interview: Ron Thomas

Clemson University has one of the most successful packaging science programs in the nation. The University offers bachelor's and master's degree programs in Packaging Science. Professor Ron Thomas, Ph.D. and Chair of Clemson's Department of Packaging Science, was kind enough to discuss his program with the editors of *They Teach That in College!?*

Q. Please briefly describe your program.

A. Packaging science is a blend of science and technology, design, marketing, and business principles. We consider the program to be highly applied in nature, and our goal is to produce industry-ready graduates.

Q. What types of students enter your program? What are their career goals and interests?

A. Students with aptitude in math (especially physics) and science (especially chemistry) and/or engineering are typically interested in this program. These students are typically interested in applied science and engineering and are looking for practical careers in industry.

Q. What types of companies employ packaging science graduates?

A. Packaging is a $115 billion business in the United States, and jobs are quite plentiful for our graduates. We consider that most all companies are in the packaging business since everyone who has a product packages it for distribution. These are "user" companies. All major food and medical companies fall into this category. The producers, or "converters," such as Sealed Air, Mitsubishi, Sonoco, International Paper, Georgia-Pacific, Smurfit, etc., are not as well known by name, but are also major employers. Starting salaries are $45,000 to $50,000.

Q. What are the key skills that packaging science students need to learn in your program to be successful in their careers?

A. As mentioned earlier, the key skill for success is the ability to blend many different disciplines. This is a significant niche that most companies have difficulty filling, and this is one of the major reasons the industry sought to get a program going at Clemson.

Q. Does your school offer any co-op opportunities?

A. Co-ops are mandatory in our program. They are typically of six months' duration, and we assist students in finding their co-ops by hosting co-op fairs on campus. Industries come to campus and interview the students. The students are paid $16 to $20 per hour on average.

Q. What advice do you offer students as they complete their degrees and look for jobs?

A. Students seeking jobs should be flexible about location and quickly get some experience. With a couple years of experience, the job market is even better. Also, there is a global market out there, and students should be prepared and willing to travel.

Q. What is the future for your program and packaging science in general?

A. Our program continues to grow, and packaging science is established as a legitimate academic discipline. There are many schools now offering courses and concentrations in packaging throughout the country, and I expect more schools to become involved. Clemson University considers our program to be of great significance and continually promotes our programs and provides the faculty we need to be successful.

Paper Science and Engineering

Papermaking is one of the oldest industries known to man—wood-based papermaking can be traced to ancient China. Today, it is considered a science and involves more than the manufacture of raw paper. Paper scientists and engineers are responsible for finding new uses for paper products, and better and more affordable ways to produce paper, tissue, and other natural fiber products. As *process engineers,* they may work to perfect the recycling of paper and water and other materials used in the papermaking process. As *research scientists,* they may extract and work with the various components found in wood or generated by the papermaking process that can be used to create medicines, detergents, and many other goods. Or perhaps they can create new paper products that are compatible with today's high speed, four-color printers. Graduates of paper science and paper engineering programs may also work in the paper industry in sales, management, and marketing. Degrees in paper science and engineering are available at all academic levels.

Typical Classes:

- > Pulp and Paper Manufacturing
- > Paper Physics Fundamentals
- > Converting and Coating
- > Water Quality and Regulations
- > Recycling
- > Wastewater Engineering
- > Surface and Wet End Science
- > Solid Waste Treatment
- > Process Engineering and Design
- > Vector and Multivariate Calculus
- > Carbohydrate and Lignin Chemistry

Potential Employers:

- > Paper companies
- > Chemical suppliers
- > Consultants
- > Equipment suppliers
- > Governmental agencies

Available At:

The following list of schools offering programs in paper science and paper engineering is not exhaustive. For more programs, visit http://www.abet.org/accrediteac.asp or http://www.paperonweb.com/school.htm.

Georgia Institute of Technology
Institute of Paper Science and Technology
500 10th Street, NW
Atlanta, GA 30332-0620
404/894-5700
http://www.ipst.gatech.edu/degree_progs/index.html
Degrees available: Master's degree, doctorate degree

Miami University
Department of Paper and Chemical Engineering
Gaskill Hall
Oxford, OH 45056
513/529-2200
paper@muohio.edu
http://www.eas.muohio.edu/pse
Degrees available: Bachelor's degree, master's degree

University of Minnesota
Department of Bio-based Products
Kaufert Lab
2004 Folwell Avenue
St. Paul, MN 55108
612/624-8798
http://www.cnr.umn.edu/BP/courses/masters.php
Degrees available: Certificate, master's degree (both are online programs)

State University of New York
Department of Paper Science and Engineering
1 Forestry Drive, Walters Hall
Syracuse, NY 13210
315/470-6501
paperscience@esf.edu
http://www.esf.edu/pse
Degrees available: Bachelor's degree, master's degree, doctorate degree

North Carolina State University
Department of Wood and Paper Science
PO Box 8005
Raleigh, NC 27695
919/515-5807
http://natural-resources.ncsu.edu/wps/pp/index.htm
Degrees available: Bachelor's degree, master's degree, doctorate
degree

Tacoma Community College
6501 South 19th Street
Tacoma, WA 98466
253/566-5000
http://www.tacomacc.edu/inst_dept/science/programs.asp
Degrees available: Associate degree (preparatory for transfer to a
paper science or engineering program at a four-year school)

University of Washington
College of Forest Resources
PO Box 352100
Seattle, WA 98195-2100
http://www.cfr.washington.edu/Acad/undergrad/pse/pse_reqs.htm
Degrees available: Bachelor's degree, master's degree, doctorate
degree

Western Michigan University
Department of Paper Engineering, Chemical Engineering, and
Imaging
A-250 Parkview Campus
Kalamazoo, MI 49008
http://www.wmich.edu/ppse
Degrees available: Bachelor's degree, master's degree, doctorate
degree

Did You Know?

Paper, according to the American Forest and Paper Association, is used in a variety of products, including writing paper, tissue, paper bags, cardboard boxes, milk cartons, masking tape, car filters, tea bags, camera film, and construction products (insulation, gypsum wallboard, roofing paper, flooring, padding, and sound-absorbing materials).

University of Wisconsin-Stevens Point
College of Natural Resources
2100 Main Street, Science Building, Room D-284
Stevens Point, WI 54481-3897
715/346-0123
papersci@uwsp.edu
http://www.uwsp.edu/papersci/Undergraduate/deptdesc.html
Degrees available: Bachelor's degree

For More Information:

American Forest and Paper Association
1111 19th Street, NW, Suite 800
Washington, DC 20036
800/878-8878
info@afandpa.org
http://www.afandpa.org

Society of Wood Science and Technology
One Gifford Pinchot Drive
Madison, WI 53726-2398
608/231-9347
http://www.swst.org

Perfusion Technology

One of the most important medical advances in history was the invention of the heart-lung machine, which serves as a patient's heart and lungs by artificially circulating their blood when the function of the patient's own heart is stopped during surgery. The operation of this lifesaving machine is the responsibility of the *perfusionist,* also known as a *cardiovascular perfusionist,* a technician who sets up and monitors the machine during surgery. Perfusionists may also be responsible for other life-support devices, and generally assist the surgical team as necessary. Because of the nature of their work, perfusionists must be trained in the biological science of artificial circulation, as well as in the mechanical functioning of the heart-lung machine and any other device they operate and monitor during medical procedures. Training to become a perfusionist is available from one of 21 schools in the United States; these schools are accredited by the Commission on Accreditation of Allied Health Education Programs.

Typical Courses:

> Basic Surgery and Monitoring
> Cardiac Anatomy and Physiology
> Immunotoxicology
> Biostatistics
> Principles of Pharmacology
> Perfusion Techniques
> Systems Physiology
> Cardiovascular Pharmacology
> Science, Society, and Ethics

Potential Employers:

> Hospitals
> U.S. military

Available At:

The following list of colleges that offer degrees in perfusion technology is not exhaustive.For a complete list of perfusion technology programs, visit http://www.caahep.org/programs.aspx or http://www.perfusion.com/perfusion/hidden/school_results.asp?Display=1.

University of Arizona
Circulatory Science Perfusion Program
501 North Campbell Avenue, PO Box 245071
Tucson, AZ 85724
520/626-6494
http://www.perfusion.arizona.edu
Degrees available: Master's degree

Barry University
School of Natural and Health Sciences
Cardiovascular Perfusion Program
11300 Northeast 2nd Avenue
Miami Shores, FL 33161-6695
305/899-3214
cvp@mail.barry.edu
http://www.barry.edu/snhs/BSprograms/cardioPerfusion/default.htm
Degrees available: Bachelor's degree

Cleveland State University
Cleveland Clinic Foundation School of Perfusion
9500 Euclid Avenue
Cleveland, OH 44195-5001
216/444-3895
http://www.csuohio.edu/healthsci/Perfusion.htm
Degrees available: Bachelor's degree, master's degree,
graduate certificate

Medical University of South Carolina
College of Health Professions
PO Box 250964
151B Rutledge Avenue
Charleston, SC 29425
843/792-2298
http://www.musc.edu/chp/cp
Degrees available: Bachelor's degree

Milwaukee School of Engineering
1025 North Broadway Street, S-355B
Milwaukee, WI 53202
414/277-7561
http://www.msoe.edu/grad/msp
Degrees available: Master's degree

University of Nebraska Medical Center
School of Allied Health Professions
985155 Nebraska Medical Center
Omaha, NE 68198-5155
402/559-7227
http://www.unmc.edu/dept/alliedhealth/cpe/index.cfm?conref=11
Degrees available: Master's degree

State University of New York Upstate Medical University
College of Health Professions
750 East Adams Street
Syracuse, NY 13210
315/464-6933
CVP@upstate.edu
http://www.upstate.edu/chp/cp
Degrees available: Bachelor's degree

Ohio State University
School of Allied Medical Professions
453 West Tenth Street, 152 Atwell Hall
Columbus, OH 43210
614/292-7261, ext. 2
riley.267@osu.edu
http://amp.osu.edu/ct/1348.cfm
Degrees available: Bachelor's degree, master's degree

Quinnipiac University
School of Health Sciences
275 Mount Carmel Avenue
Hamden, CT 06518-1940
http://www.quinnipiac.edu/x1903.xml
Degrees available: Post-baccalaureate certificate

Rush University
Cardiovascular Perfusion Program
600 South Paulina, Suite 1021D
Chicago, IL 60612
http://www.rushu.rush.edu/perfusion
Degrees available: Master's degree

For More Information:

American Academy of Cardiovascular Perfusion
PO Box 3596
Allentown, PA 18106-0596
http://members.aol.com/OfficeAACP/home.html

American Society of Extra-Corporeal Technology
2209 Dickens Road, PO Box 11086
Richmond, VA 23230-1086
http://www.amsect.org

Perfusion.com
http://www.perfusion.com

Interview: Robin Sutton

Robin Sutton is the Director of the Cardiovascular Perfusion Program at Rush University in Chicago, Illinois. She discussed her program and the education of perfusion technology students with the editors of *They Teach That in College!?*

Q. Please provide an overview of your program.

A. Our program is a 20-month full-time program and awards an entry-level master's degree upon completion. An entry-level master's degree means that a student enters the program with a bachelor's degree, but not necessarily in perfusion. When they graduate from the program they will be eligible to sit for the national certification exam and will be eligible for state licensure. The first three quarters of the program are primarily classroom, and the last four quarters involve research and clinical rotations.

Q. What high school subjects/activities should students focus on to be successful in this major?

A. Interested students should focus on science and mathematics. As in most medical fields, students should take high school courses that will prepare them for college courses in chemistry, human physiology, pathology, pharmacology, research, and biostatistics. Since operating the heart-lung machine involves pumping blood through plastic tubing and using devices that transfer heat, oxygen, and carbon dioxide, a physics course focusing on fluid dynamics and gas laws is beneficial.

Q. What are the most important personal and professional qualities for perfusion technology majors?

A. Because the program is academically challenging, we look for individuals who have good grades in mathematics and science. Secondly, we look for individuals who have a good understanding of what a perfusionist does, which can be accomplished by researching on the Internet or, better yet, talking to a perfusionist. We also look for students who have a good attitude, attention to detail, interpersonal skills, and who are dependable, organized, self-confident, and good problem solvers.

Q. What educational level is typically required for perfusion technology graduates to land good jobs in the industry?

A. The minimal criteria for entry into the profession is a bachelor's degree. About one-third of the programs in the country award a bachelors degree, about one-third award a master's degree, and the rest require a bachelor's degree as a prerequisite and award a certificate upon completion. We offer a master's degree because we feel this will provide more opportunities for career advancement.

Q. How will the field of perfusion technology change in the future?

A. New technology will be emerging in the areas of heart transplant and artificial hearts.

Personal Fitness Training

Personal trainers are key players in the fitness industry, helping clients achieve personal exercise goals, lose weight, and rehabilitate from injury. But there is a great variance in training and skill levels in this fast-growing occupation. While physical education majors have been offered at colleges and universities for years, no baccalaureate training for personal trainers has been available—until now. Purdue University-West Lafayette is the first four-year degree program in the United States to offer a concentration in personal training. The goal of the program, which was founded in 2005, is to improve the professional standing of personal trainers and prepare students for certification examinations offered by the American College of Sports Medicine. In addition to studying biomechanics, physiology, neurology, functional anatomy, and related concepts, students also focus on business and career development skills, which will help them to improve their management abilities and start their own personal training businesses. Employment of fitness workers is expected to grow by 35 percent through 2012, according to the U.S. Department of Labor.

204

Typical Courses:

> Human Anatomy and Physiology
> Essentials of Nutrition
> Methods of Health Promotion and Education
> Health and Fitness Program Management
> Health Screening and Fitness Evaluation and Prescription
> Anatomical Foundations of Human Performance
> Principles of Motor Learning and Development
> Exercise Testing and Prescription for Special Populations
> Exercise Physiology
> Sport and Exercise Physiology
> Clinical Practice in Personal Training
> Business Issues for Personal Trainers

Potential Employers:

> Private and commercial health clubs
> Corporate fitness centers
> Aerobics studios
> Rehabilitation centers

> Hospitals
> Colleges and universities
> Community wellness programs
> Personal training studios
> Physical therapy clinics
> YMCAs

Available At:

Purdue University-West Lafayette
Department of Health and Kinesiology
100 North University Street
West Lafayette, IN 47906-2067
http://tholian.sla.purdue.edu/academic/hk/hkadvising/PFT.htm
Degrees available: Bachelor's degree

For More Information:

American College of Sports Medicine
PO Box 1440
Indianapolis, IN 46206-1440
317/637-9200
http://www.acsm.org

American Council on Exercise
4851 Paramount Drive
San Diego, CA 92123
800/825-3636
http://www.acefitness.org

American Fitness Professionals and Associates
PO Box 214
Ship Bottom, NJ 08008
800/494-7782
afpa@afpafitness.com
http://www.afpafitness.com

IDEA Health and Fitness Association
10455 Pacific Center Court
San Diego, CA 92121-4339
http://www.ideafit.com

Petroleum Engineering

Travel storm-tossed oceans, frozen tundra, steep mountainsides, and unending deserts of the world in search for the black gold that is known as petroleum. Petroleum engineers explore, drill, and produce the production of oil, as well as gas and other natural resources, that are imperative to the functioning of our transportation systems and industries. As a petroleum engineer, you'll not only work to meet the demand for safe affordable energy, but you may also work in perfecting petroleum by-products such as plastics, textiles, and medicine. Placement of bachelor of science graduates (the minimum educational requirement for a career as a petroleum engineer) is almost 100 percent, and the average starting salary, according to the National Association of Colleges and Employers, was $55,987 in 2003. A master's degree in petroleum engineering or a related field is required for top positions in this field.

206

Typical Courses:

> Chemistry, Physics, and Geology
> Petrophysics
> Applied Reservoir Analysis
> Drilling Engineering
> Production Systems Engineering
> Natural Gas Engineering
> Transient Pressure Analysis
> Drilling and Completion Fluids
> Rock and Fluid Properties
> Principles of Well Testing and Analysis

Potential Employers:

> Major oil companies
> Independent oil exploration, production, and service companies
> Colleges and universities
> Consulting companies
> Governmental agencies

Available At:

The following list of schools offering programs in petroleum engineering is not exhaustive. For more programs, visit the following website, http://www.spe.org.

University of Alaska-Fairbanks
425 Duckering Building, PO Box 755880
Fairbanks, AK 99775-5880
907/474-7734
fyipete@uaf.edu
http://www.uaf.edu/petrol
Degrees available: Bachelor's degree, master's degree

University of Kansas
Department of Chemical and Petroleum Engineering
1530 West 15th Street, 4132 Learned Hall
Lawrence, KS 66045-7609
785/864-4965
cpe@ku.edu
http://www.cpe.engr.ku.edu
Degrees available: Bachelor's degree, master's degree

University of Louisiana-Lafayette
Department of Engineering
Martin Hall, Room 126, PO Box 44690
Lafayette, LA 70504-4690
337/482-5750
petroleum@lousiana.edu
http://petroleum.louisiana.edu
Degrees available: Bachelor's degree

Louisiana State University
Craft and Hawkins Department of Petroleum Engineering
3516 CEBA Building
Baton Rouge, LA 70803
225/578-5215
http://www.pete.lsu.edu
Degrees available: Bachelor's degree, master's degree,
doctorate degree

Marietta College
Department of Petroleum Engineering
215 Fifth Street, 201 Brown Building
Marietta, OH 45750-4017
740/376-4775
prtr@maruetta.edu
http://www.marietta.edu/~petr
Degrees available: Bachelor's degree

University of Missouri-Rolla
Department of Geological Sciences and Engineering

1870 Miner Circle, 125 McNutt Hall
Rolla, MO 65409-0140
573/341-4616
rocks@umr.edu
http://www.umr.edu/~pet-eng
Degrees available: Bachelor's degree, master's degree, doctorate degree

Montana Tech of the University of Montana
Department of Petroleum Engineering
1300 West Park Street
Butte, MT 59701
406/496-4101
http://www.mtech.edu/cf_prototypes/admission/programs.
php?Program_ID=BSPT
Degrees available: Bachelor's degree, master's degree

New Mexico Tech
Department of Petroleum Engineering
801 Leroy Place, MSEC 300A
Socorro, NM 87801
505/835-5412
http://www.nmt.edu/~petro
Degree levels offered: Bachelor's degree, master's degree, doctorate degree

University of Oklahoma
Mewbourne School of Petroleum and Geological Engineering
T-301 Sarkeys Energy Center
100 Boyde Street
Norman, OK 73019-1003
405/325-2921
mpge@ou.edu
http://www.ou.edu/mewbourneschool
Degrees available: Bachelor's degree, master's degree, doctorate degree

Penn State University
Petroleum and Natural Gas Engineering
115 Hosler Building
University Park, PA 16802
814/865-6082
pnge@ems.psu.edu
http://www.pnge.psu.edu/undergradprog.htm
Degrees available: Bachelor's degree, master's degree, doctorate degree

Did You Know?

Oil isn't used just as an energy source for our homes and vehicles. In fact, according to the American Petroleum Institute, it's used in ways you've never imagined! Indeed, oil is used to make antihistamines, clothing, computers, garbage bags, heart valve replacements, life jackets, perfumes, roofing, soft contact lenses, telephones, toothpaste, and umbrellas.

University of Pittsburgh
Department of Chemical and Petroleum Engineering
1249 Benedum Hall
Pittsburgh, PA 15261
412/624-9630
ChE@engr.pitt.edu
http://www.engr.pitt.edu/chemical/index.html
Degrees available: Bachelor's degree, master's degree, doctorate degree

University of Southern California
Mork Family Department of Chemical Engineering and Materials Science
925 Bloom Walk-HED 316
Los Angeles, CA 90089-1211
213/740-0322
peteng@usc.edu
http://chems.usc.edu/academics/graduate.html
Degrees available: Bachelor's degree, master's degree, graduate certificate

Stanford University
Department of Petroleum Engineering
367 Panama Street, Green Earth Sciences Building, Room 065
Stanford, CA 94305-2220
650/723-4744
peteng@pangea.stanford.edu
http://ekofisk.stanford.edu
Degrees available: Bachelor's degree, master's degree, doctorate degree

Texas A&M University
Department of Petroleum Engineering
3116 TAMU

507 Richardson Building
College Station, TX 77843-3116
979/845-2241
info@pe.tamu.edu
http://pumpjack.tamu.edu
Degrees available: Bachelor's degree, master's degree, doctorate
degree

University of Texas-Austin
Petroleum and Geosystems Engineering
1 University Station C0300
Austin, TX 78712-0228
512/471-3161
pgeundergradoffice@mail.utexas.edu
http://www.pge.utexas.edu
Degrees available: Bachelor's degree, master's degree, doctorate
degree

Texas Tech University
Petroleum Engineering Department
8th & Canton Avenue
Lubbock, TX 79409-3111
806/742-3573
http://www.pe.ttu.edu
Degrees available: Bachelor's degree, master's degree, doctorate
degree

University of Tulsa
Department of Petroleum Engineering
600 South College Avenue
Tulsa, OK 74104
918/631-2533
http://www.pe.utulsa.edu
Degrees available: Bachelor's degree, master's degree, doctorate
degree

West Virginia University
College of Engineering and Mineral Resources
PO Box 6070
Morgantown, WV 26506-6070
304/293-7682
http://www.pnge.cemr.wvu.edu
Degrees available: Bachelor's degree, master's degree, doctorate
degree

For More Information:

American Petroleum Institute
1220 L Street, NW
Washington, DC 20005-4070
202/682-8000
info@api.org
http://www.api.org

American Society for Engineering Education
1818 N Street, NW, Suite 600
Washington, DC 20036-2479
202/331-3500
http://www.asee.org

Junior Engineering Technical Society, Inc.
1420 King Street, Suite 405
Alexandria, VA 22314
703/548-5387
info@jets.org
http://www.jets.org

Society of Petroleum Engineers
PO Box 833836
Richardson, TX 75083-3836
972/952-9393
spedal@spe.org
http://www.spe.org

Plastics Engineering/Science

Look around and you will see plastics in almost every aspect of your life. Plastics are used in health care (e.g., surgical gloves, open MRI machines, prosthetic devices), waste treatment, electronics, construction, agriculture, and in everyday life (e.g., bottles, food storage, product packaging, and countless other uses). Someday, according to Plasticscar.org, plastics may make up a large percentage of the interior and exterior of cars and other vehicles. In short, the sky's the limit for students interested in careers in plastics. *Plastics engineers,* who design and develop plastic products, typically have associate or bachelor's degrees in plastic or polymer engineering, materials engineering, chemical engineering, industrial engineering, manufacturing engineering, or a related field. *Plastics technicians,* who assist plastics engineers, typically have some postsecondary training or an associate degree.

212

Typical Courses:

> Overview of the Plastics Industry
> Polymer Processing Survey
> Mathematics
> Chemistry
> 3D CAD and Modeling
> Manufacturing Processes
> Injection Molding
> Mold Design/Maintenance
> Industrial Blow Molding
> Extrusion
> Polymer Testing

Potential Employers:

> Aerospace industry
> Building and construction industry
> Electronics industry
> Packaging industry
> Transportation industry
> Virtually any industry that uses plastics in its products

Available At:

The following list of schools offering programs in plastics engineering and related fields is not exhaustive. For more programs, visit the following websites: http://www.plasticsindustry.org/outreach/institutions and http://www.abet.org/schoolareatac.asp#O.

Clemson University
School of Materials Science and Engineering
161 Sirrine Hall
Clemson, SC 29634
864/656-3176
http://mse.clemson.edu/htm/degrees/poly_tex_chem.htm
Degrees available: Bachelor's degree

College of DuPage
Plastics Technology Program
425 Fawell Boulevard, IC 3028
Glen Ellyn, IL 60137-6599
630/942-4343
http://www.cod.edu/academic/acadprog/occ_voc/PlasAcad.htm
Degrees available: Associate degree

University of Massachusetts-Lowell
Department of Plastics Engineering
One University Avenue
Lowell, MA 01854
978/934-3435
http://plastics.caeds.eng.uml.edu
Degrees available: Bachelor's degree, master's degree, doctorate degree

Did You Know?

More than 1.4 million people work in the U.S. plastics industry, according to the Society of the Plastics Industry. The industry is one of the largest in the United States.

Pennsylvania College of Technology
Plastics and Polymer Technology Department
Breuder Advanced Technology and Health Sciences Center
Room E134
One College Avenue
Williamsport, PA 17701
570/327-4520
plastics@pct.edu
http://www.pct.edu
Degrees available: Associate degree, bachelor's degree

Pennsylvania State University
Behrend College
Plastics Engineering Technology
5091 Station Road
Erie, PA 16563
814/898-6482
http://www.pserie.psu.edu/academic/engineering/degrees/plet
Degrees available: Bachelor's degree

Pittsburg State University
Plastics Engineering Technology Program
Kansas Technology Center, Room W223
1701 South Broadway
Pittsburg, KS 66762
620/235-4350
etech@pittstate.edu
http://www.pittstate.edu/etech/plastics.html
Degrees available: Bachelor's degree

University of Southern California
Mork Family Department of Chemical Engineering and
Materials Science
3651 Watt Way, VHE 602
Los Angeles, CA 90089-0241
http://chems.usc.edu
Degrees available: Bachelor's degree, master's degree, doctorate
degree

University of Southern Mississippi
School of Polymers and High Performance Materials
118 College Drive, #1007
Hattiesburg, MS 39406-0001
http://www.psrc.usm.edu
Degrees available: Bachelor's degree, master's degree, doctorate
degree

Western Washington University
Department of Engineering Technology
516 High Street
Bellingham, WA 98225-9086
360/650-3380
http://www.etec.wwu.edu
Degrees available: Bachelor's degree

University of Wisconsin-Stout
College of Technology Engineering and Management
332 Fryklund Hall
Menomonie, WI 54751-0790
http://www.uwstout.edu/programs/bset
Degrees available: Bachelor's degree

For More Information:

American Plastics Council
1300 Wilson Boulevard
Arlington, VA 22209
800/243-5790
http://www.plastics.org

Plastics Institute of America, Inc.
University of Massachusetts-Lowell
333 Aiken Street
Lowell, MA 01854-3686
978/934-3130
info@plasticsinstitute.org
http://pia.caeds.eng.uml.edu

Society of Plastics Engineers
14 Fairfield Drive, PO Box 403
Brookfield, CT 06804-0403
203/775-0471
info@4spe.org
http://www.4spe.org

Society of the Plastics Industry
1667 K Street, NW, Suite 1000
Washington, DC 20006
202/974-5200
http://www.socplas.org

Interview: Robert Malloy

Dr. Robert Malloy is the Chairman of the Department of Plastics Engineering at the University of Massachusetts Lowell. He discussed the program and the education of plastics engineering students with the editors of *They Teach That in College!?*

Q. Please provide an overview of your program.

A. The Plastics Engineering Department is an internationally recognized leader in plastics engineering education. Founded in 1954, we offer the only BS Plastics Engineering program in the United States that is accredited by the Accrediting Board for Engineering and Technology Programs. More than 3,000 graduates are working in the plastics industry in leadership positions worldwide. Programs of study include:

✓ Bachelor of Science Degree in Plastics Engineering
✓ Bachelor of Science in Plastics Engineering with a Business Administration Minor
✓ Five-Year Bachelor of Science/Master of Science Program in Plastics Engineering
✓ Master's Degree Program in Plastics Engineering
✓ Doctor of Engineering Degree in Plastics Engineering

The program combines hands-on laboratory experiences relevant to the industry, with the fundamental theory found in courses of mathematics, science, and engineering to produce a well-rounded curriculum. Constant feedback from industry and alumni enable us to stay on the cutting edge of plastics manufacturing and design technologies.

The Department has 15,000 square feet of dedicated laboratory space. Students are exposed to all of the major plastics manufacturing, design, and testing technologies.

Q. What high school subjects/activities should students focus on to be successful in this major?

A. Students who have an interest in chemistry, physics, and math usually do well in the plastics engineering major. Students should participate in design- or materials-related projects whenever possible.

216

Q. What are the most important personal and professional qualities for plastics engineering majors?

A. Some subtle differences from traditional engineering programs are: 1) willingness to really do things; students need to be comfortable with both practical and theoretical sides of a problem more than other majors; 2) a more diverse set of academic interests—especially an interest in understanding the connection between chemistry and mechanical engineering. As a family of materials, I consider plastics the most "versatile" materials on Earth. Our plastics engineering program has a great deal of chemistry so that students develop an understanding of why plastics materials behave or perform as they do. Our students should be able to look at the chemical structure of a plastic and understand how it will behave (i.e., predict its properties).

Q. How will the field of plastics engineering change in the future?

A. The plastics industry is very dynamic. New materials and processes are being developed all the time. We are beginning to see more commercial plastics being developed from renewable resources and growth in the area of biodegradable plastics and plastics recycling, especially for packaging applications. The area of medical plastics is also growing rapidly. New medical devices for less-invasive surgery are largely made from plastics. Other items such as bio-absorbable bone repair screws and artificial joints continue to evolve. More plastics in automobiles reduces weight leading to improved fuel economy.

Globalization is always a concern when it comes to product manufacturing; however, plastics part design and manufacturing in the U.S. maintains good long term prospects.

Two other trends: 1) an increasing emphasis on product leadership and project management (engineers are needed to manage entire commercial processes), and 2) a ratcheting of skills up the technology ladder (to lower costs, to improve consistency, and to enable more advanced products and thereby avoid commoditization).

For more information on our programs, visit http://plastics.uml.edu.

Producer, Film and Television

Actor, director, cinematographer, special effects artist . . . these are the typical options people think of when considering careers in film or television. But the career of producer should also be considered by students with business acumen, ambition, a love of film and/or television, and an artistic sensibility. According to the Producers Guild of America, producers "initiate, coordinate, supervise, and control . . . all aspects of the motion-picture and/or television production process, including creative, financial, technological, and administrative [duties]." In the past, producers typically learned their trade via on-the-job experience or by working their way up through a variety of other positions in the industry. Today, college programs have been created to train producers to enter this demanding, yet exciting, career. Although bachelor's degree programs are available in producing, most industry experts feel that a graduate degree in production offers students the best opportunity to break into this highly competitive field.

218

Typical Courses:

> Film History
> Film and Television Production
> Film and Television Post Production
> Planning the Independent Film Production
> Production Management
> Film and Television Financing
> Entertainment Law
> Marketing/Distribution/Exhibition
> Independent Feature Filmmaking
> Business

Potential Employers:

> Television production companies
> Film production companies
> Film and television studios

Available At:

University of California-Los Angeles
Producers Program
102 East Melnitz Hall, Box 951622

Los Angeles, CA 90095-1622
info@tft.ucla.edu
http://www.tft.ucla.edu/producers/start.htm
Degrees available: Master's degree

Chapman University
Dodge College of Film and Media Arts
One University Drive
DeMille Hall, Room 127
Orange, CA 92866
714/997-6765
DodgeCollege@chapman.edu
http://ftv.chapman.edu/prospective/undergraduate/production.cf
m and http://ftv.chapman.edu/prospective/grad/producing.cfm
Degrees available: Bachelor's degree, master's degree

Columbia University
School of the Arts
513 Dodge Hall
212/854-2815
film@columbia.edu
http://www.app.cc.columbia.edu/art/app/arts/film/viewProgram.jsp
Degrees available: Master's degree

For More Information:

Producers Guild of America
8530 Wilshire Boulevard, Suite 450
Beverly Hills, CA 90211
info@producersguild.org
http://www.producersguild.org

Interview: Denise Mann

Denise Mann is an Assistant Professor and Head of the Producers Program at the University of California-Los Angeles (UCLA). Students who complete this unique two-year program receive a Master of Fine Arts and are well prepared for careers as producers in the film and television industries. Mann discussed her program and the career of producer with the editors of *They Teach That in College!?*

Q. Tell us about your program.

A. One of the defining features of the University of California-Los Angeles Producers Program and a central reason for its national and international prominence is its prestigious faculty comprised largely of established industry professionals. Our faculty members include studio heads, heads of agencies, networks, and major producers, attorneys, and other prominent industry leaders. The unique strength of the Producers Program is its ability to provide rigorous and up-to-date creative and business courses on a range of topics having to do with the contemporary Hollywood entertainment industry.

Q. What personal qualities do students need to be successful in your program?

A. We encourage those who apply to the Producers Program to come to the table with a strong educational background and good grades; however, that is true of most graduate programs. Given how demanding our program is and how competitive it is to secure jobs in the Hollywood entertainment industry, we are also looking for individuals who bring a great deal of energy and ambition to the table. Additionally, prospective students should have made every effort to educate themselves about this complex and demanding field by reading the industry trades (*Daily Variety* or *Hollywood Reporter*), watching as many films as possible, reading as many screenplays as possible, and taking film history survey courses (American film history, German film history, French film history, etc.) at their university so that they are familiar both with Hollywood films made before the 1980s and also with as many films made outside the United States as possible.

When they are juniors or seniors in college, students are encouraged to intern at one of the hundreds of Hollywood-based development-production companies, at one of the major talent agencies, at a management company, at a studio (in development, marketing, distribution, or some other department), at one of the networks, or at one of the cable companies. Most students without a background in film think the only way to proceed is to work in production as a production assistant on the set of a film, television show, commercial, or music video. By all means, knowing production is an important part of a producer's learning curve; however, additionally, students who are considering a career in producing should consider interning in development at one of the major production companies, management companies, or literary agencies that represent writers. By supporting the efforts of the executives and producers who work long hours inside these offices to find and develop great material, students start to acquire the necessary story sense and strategic business skills that go into producing. (To help familiarize yourself with the range of companies engaged in development, you may wish to explore one of the many published or online directories devoted to listing studios, networks, production companies, and the company credits, such as the *Hollywood Creative Directory,* Internet Movie Database, etc.). Interning at these companies not only gives students a basic understanding of who's who in the industry and the hierarchies involved, but it also gives them a sense of the volume of screenplays submitted that never see the light of day. By reading and evaluating large numbers of screenplays, students start to assess what makes certain screenplays stand out and start to gather the attention of established producers, talent, directors, financiers, and distributors. Most of the film and television companies offering internships are located in either Los Angeles or New York, but occasionally you can find them in other major cities that are involved in feature film production. Most of the major universities offering film programs in Los Angeles and New York, in particular, offer internship opportunities to non-residents during their summer sessions.

Finally, students who want to enter producing can continue to learn on their own by reading as many screenplays as they can get their hands on and by evaluating what makes them work. We are not looking for "closet writers" in the Producers Program, but rather, we are looking for producers with a keen eye for great stories. You should be educating yourself not only about how the marketplace functions, but about how you can become a more productive collaborator and support figure for talented new writers and directors. Develop a sense of which projects you'd like to produce if you were given the chance. To support this effort, start making friends with screenwriters now and learn how to help them become better at what they do best-writing. Start watching movies and reading screenplays and look for ways in which they both adhere to and/or provide innovative departures from the Hollywood conventions of genre and story structure.

Q. What advice would you offer students as they complete your program and look for jobs?

A. The advice I offer students after they complete the Producers Program is to continue honing the story and strategic-thinking skills they acquired while in the graduate program. Most students who graduate from the Producers Program pursue assistant-level jobs at agencies, production companies, studios, and networks. The advantage of going to graduate school is that you will be much more likely to advance up the ranks efficiently because you will have a more in-depth understanding of the whole industry. Students in the Producers Program have an advantage over individuals who go into jobs immediately because they are gleaning insights from industry professionals who have spent several decades sharpening their craft. The other thing I tell both current and graduating students from the Producers Program is that producers are only as good as the material to which they are attached. Some students make the mistake of thinking all they have to do is come up with a great idea for a movie. That's only the first step. The really hard work begins when you start working with a writer to turn the idea into a viable screenplay, one that will attract talented actors to play the key roles and that will inspire a talented director to commit several years of his or her life to turning it into a movie. Finally, producers must always be thinking about the audience. They must ask themselves "who will pay the price to go see my film?" Inevitably, producing represents a balance of artistic and commercial agendas.

Prosthetics and Orthotics

Prosthetists and *orthotists* are allied health professionals who work with prostheses and orthoses—such as braces, helmets, and artificial limbs—that help improve the lives of individuals in need of such assistive devices. They work as members of a patient's rehabilitation team, along with physicians, nurses, physical and/or occupational therapists, dieticians, and social workers. The prosthetist/orthotist may be involved with evaluating the individual in need of an orthosis or prosthesis, and the original design, building, and fitting of the device for that individual. Prosthetists and orthotists often have the opportunity to work in varied environments, spending time with individuals in need of assistive devices, as well working in the lab to create new orthoses and prostheses. In addition, this allied health profession offers a variety of exciting employment opportunities available at different levels—practitioners, assistants, and technicians—depending on a person's educational background. Practitioners require a bachelor's degree, post-baccalaureate certificate, or a master's degree. Assistants and technicians require an associate degree.

Typical Courses:

> Health Care Systems and Perspectives
> Orthotics and Prosthetics
> Public Health
> Pathophysiology for Prosthetics and Orthotics
> Health Behavior
> Biomechanics and Kinesiology for Prosthetics and Orthotics
> Below and Above Knee Prosthetics
> Normal and Pathological Gait
> Materials Science and Applied Anatomy in Prosthetics & Orthotics
> Upper Limb Prosthetics
> Research in Health Sciences

Potential Employers:

> Hospitals
> Rehabilitation centers
> U.S. military

Available At:

Orthotic and Prosthetic Practitioner Programs

California State University
College of Health and Human Services
27402 Aliso Viejo Parkway
Aliso Viejo, CA 92656
800/344-5484
oandp@csudh.edu
http://www.csudh.edu/oandp
Degrees available: Bachelor's degree, post-baccalaureate certificate

Century College
Orthotic and Prosthetic Programs
3300 Century Avenue North
White Bear Lake, MN 55110
651/773-1700
http://www.century.edu/orthoticprosthetic/opsaoverview.aspx
Degrees available: Post-baccalaureate certificate

Eastern Michigan University
106 Welch Hall
Ypsilanti, MI 48197
734/487-0090
http://www.fedel.com/emu2/oandp
Degrees available: Post-baccalaureate certificate (This program is still in the development stage. Check with the University regarding its status.)

Georgia Institute of Technology
School of Applied Physiology
281 Ferst Drive
Atlanta, GA 30332-0356
404/894-7658
joy.daniell@ap.gatech.edu
http://www.ap.gatech.edu/mspo/index.htm
Degrees available: Master's degree

Newington Certificate Program in Orthotics and Prosthetics
Curtis Professional Building
181 Patricia M. Genova Drive
5th Floor East Wing
Newington, CT 06111
ncp@hanger.com
http://www.hanger.com/ncp/index.html
Degree level available: Post-baccalaureate certificate

Northwestern University
Prosthetic-Orthotic Center
345 East Superior Street, Room 1712
Chicago, IL 60611-4496
312/238-8006
v-rachel@northwestern.edu
http://www.medschool.northwestern.edu/depts/nupoc
Degrees available: Post-baccalaureate certificate

Did You Know?

More than 4.1 million Americans use orthoses (braces) for disabling conditions such as stroke, multiple sclerosis and Parkinson's Disease, as well as for orthopedic impairments due to sports activities, other physical trauma, birth defects, and advanced arthritis, according to the Centers for Disease Control and Prevention. Over the next two decades, the number of disabled patients is likely to grow to more than 42 million, according to a study prepared for the National Commission on Orthotic and Prosthetic Education. By 2005 a potential 1.3 million people could be without adequate orthotic care.

225

Rancho Los Amigos Medical Center
Orthotic Department
7450 Leeds Street
Downey, CA 90242
562/940-7655
http://www.oandp.com/resources/education/larei
Degree level available: Post-baccalaureate certificate (orthotics only)

St. Petersburg College
PO Box 13489
St. Petersburg, FL 33733-3489
727/341-3406
http://www.spcollege.edu/bachelors/op_main.php
Degrees available: Bachelor's degree (new program, accepting applications for Fall 2006)

University of Texas Southwestern Medical Center
School of Allied Health Sciences
Orthotics & Prosthetics Programs
5323 Harry Hines Boulevard

Dallas, TX 75390-9091
214/648-1580
po.sahss@utsouthwestern.edu
http://www8.utsouthwestern.edu/utsw/cda/dept28640/files/
51716.html
Degrees available: Bachelor's degree

University of Washington
Department of Rehabilitation Medicine
1959 NE Pacific Street, Box 356490
Seattle, WA 98195
206/543-3600
rehab@u.washington.edu
http://depts.washington.edu/rehab
Degrees available: Bachelor's degree

Orthotic and Prosthetic Assistant Programs
Oklahoma State University-Okmulgee
1801 East 4th Street
Okmulgee, OK 74447
918/293-5330
andrea.autaubo@okstate.edu
http://www.osu-okmulgee.edu/academics/
health_and_environmental/orthotics_and_prosthetics
Degrees available: Associate degree

Orthotic and Prosthetic Technician Programs
Baker College of Flint
O&P Technology Program
1050 West Bristol Road
Flint, MI 48507
810/766-4194
https://carina.baker.edu/PGMSO?DLV=U&DIV=HHSP&DIVT-
TL=Health%20Sciences%20Programs&DEPT=ADM
Degrees available: Associate degree

Century College
O&P Programs
3300 Century Avenue North
White Bear Lake, MN 55110
651/773-1700
http://www.century.edu/orthoticprosthetic/opsaoverview.aspx
Degrees available: Associate degree

Francis Tuttle
12777 North Rockwell Avenue
Oklahoma City, OK 73142-2789

405/717-4199
http://www.francistuttle.com/programs/details.asp?PRGID=13
Degrees available: Associate degree

Spokane Falls Community College
3410 West Fort George Wright Drive, Mail Stop 3060
Spokane, WA 99204-5288
509/533-3732
http://tech.spokanefalls.edu/OandP/
default.asp?page=Home&OP=1
Degrees available: Certificate, associate degree

For More Information:

American Academy of Orthotists and Prosthetists
526 King Street, Suite 201
Alexandria, VA 22314
703/836-0788
academy@oandp.org
http://www.oandp.org

227

American Orthotic and Prosthetic Association
330 John Carlyle Street, Suite 200
Alexandria, VA 22314
571/431-0876
info@aopanet.org
http://www.aopanet.org

National Commission on Orthotic and Prosthetic Education
330 John Carlyle Street, Suite 200
Alexandria, VA 22314
703/836-7114
info@ncope.org
http://www.ncope.org

Did You Know?

Orthotic and prosthetic graduates have a 100 percent job placement rate, according to the American Academy of Orthotists & Prosthetists.

Railroad Operations

If you ever dreamed of becoming a railroad conductor, this is the program for you! Designed to provide students with general knowledge and skills for entry-level employment in the railroad industry, this major introduces students to the history of railroading and the various railroad crafts—conducting, mechanics, electronics, and welding. Railroad operations, safety, environment, and quality are additional areas of focus. Business and technical electives provide additional opportunity for students to specialize or prepare for additional study. Most programs require students to specialize in one or more areas such as conducting, mechanics, electronics, or welding. Programs typically award certificates and associate degrees.

Typical Courses:

> History of Railroading
> Railroad Safety, Quality, and Environment
> Physics
> Mechanical Operations
> Construction Management
> Electromechanical Systems
> Industrial Safety
> Metallurgy
> Business Management

Potential Employers:

> Railroads

Available At:

Dakota County Technical College
1300 145th Street East (County Road 42)
Rosemount, MN 55068-2999
http://www.dctc.mnscu.edu/programs/rail.htm
Degrees available: Certificate

Johnson County Community College
12345 College Boulevard
Overland Park, KS 66210
http://www.jccc.edu/home/depts/4614
Degrees available: Certificate, associate degree

Did You Know?

Over the next decade, America's railroads will face an urgent shortage of qualified, well-trained men and women to operate and manage today's modern railroads. Industry experts predict that an additional 60,000 to 210,000 workers will be needed.

Modoc Railroad Academy
PO Box 432
Madison, CA 95653
mra@modocrailroadacademy.com
http://www.modocrailroadacademy.com/index.asp
Degrees available: Certificate

Sacramento City College
Department of Advanced Transportation Technology
Division of Advanced Technology
3835 Freeport Boulevard
Sacramento, CA 95822
http://www.scc.losrios.edu/programs/railroad.html
Degrees available: Certificate

St. Philip's College-Southwest Campus
800 Quintana Road
San Antonio, TX 78211
210/921-4603
http://www.accd.edu/spc/spcmain/swc/railroad.htm
Degrees available: Certificate

Tarrant County Junior College
4801 Marine Creek Parkway
Fort Worth, TX 76179
817/515-7271
http://www.tccd.edu/programs/dp.asp?dpid=229
Degrees available: Certificate

For More Information:

Association of American Railroads
50 F Street, NW
Washington, DC 20001-1564
202/639-2100
information@aar.org
http://www.aar.org

Range Management

More than 40 percent of the Earth's surface is covered by rangelands (grasslands, prairies, alpine, savanna, deserts, marshes, and certain types of forests). According to the Society for Range Management, rangeland is one of the most productive and biodiverse types of land on Earth. Range management professionals ensure that these critical ecosystems remain viable and capable of supporting livestock and wildlife, as well as provide renewable natural resources and recreation opportunities to people. This career requires knowledge of soil science, plant physiology, climatology, land management, land reclamation, and land restoration. A minimum of a bachelor's degree in range management or range science is required to work in this field. Although many schools offer coursework in range management, only about 35 colleges and universities in the United States offer degrees in range management or range science.

230

Typical Classes:

> Ranch Economics
> Range Management
> Watershed Management
> Range Improvements
> Range Analysis
> Soils
> Wildlife Management
> Range Grasses
> Range Plants
> Range Communities
> Range Ecology
> Habitat Management

Potential Employers:

> Federal agencies (such as the Natural Resources Conservation Service, Bureau of Land Management, National Park Service, Fish and Wildlife Service, and U.S. Forest Service)
> State and local government (such as fish and wildlife departments, natural resources departments, park departments, and state land agencies)
> Colleges and universities

> Private industry (such as ranch managers, mining companies, land management companies, agricultural companies)
> Nonprofit conservation organizations (such as The Nature Conservancy, the Land Trust Alliance, and The Trust for Public Land)

Available At:

The following list of schools offering programs in range management and range science is not exhaustive. For a complete list of programs, visit http://www.rangelands.org/education_universities.shtml.

University of Arizona
School of Natural Resources
Biological Sciences East, Room 325D
Tucson, AZ 85721
520/621-7260
http://ag.arizona.edu/srnr/academicprograms/index.html
Degrees available: Bachelor's degree, master's degree, doctorate degree

231

Chadron State College
Department of Applied Sciences
1000 Main Street
Chadron, NE 69337
800/CHADRON
http://www.csc.edu/ag
Degrees available: Bachelor's degree

Colorado State University
Department of Forest, Rangeland, and Watershed Stewardship
Fort Collins, CO 80523-1472
970/491-6911
frws_info@cnr.colostate.edu
http://www.warnercnr.colostate.edu/frws
Degrees available: Bachelor's degree, master's degree, doctorate degree

University of Idaho
Department of Rangeland Ecology and Management
Moscow, ID 83844-1135
208/885-6536
range@uidaho.edu
http://www.cnrhome.uidaho.edu/range
Degrees available: Bachelor's degree, master's degree

Did You Know?

There are more than one billion acres of rangeland in the United States—primarily in Alaska and the western states.

New Mexico State University
Department of Animal and Range Sciences
Box 30003, MSC 3-I
Las Cruces, NM 88003-8003
505/646-2514
ascience@nmsu.edu
http://www.nmsu.edu/~dars/deg_prog.html
Degrees available: Bachelor's degree, master's degree, doctorate degree

Oregon State University
Department of Rangeland Ecology and Management
202 Strand Agriculture Hall
Corvallis, OR 97331-2218
541/737-3341
http://oregonstate.edu/dept/range/index.php
Degrees available: Bachelor's degree

Texas A&M University
Department of Rangeland Ecology and Management
209 Animal Industries Building, 2126 TAMU
College Station, TX 77840-2126
979/845-2755
http://rangeweb.tamu.edu/extension/Index.htm
Degrees available: Bachelor's degree

Texas Tech University
Department of Range, Wildlife, and Fisheries Management
Box 42125
Lubbock, TX 79409-2125
806/742-2841
http://www.rw.ttu.edu/dept
Degrees available: Bachelor's degree, master's degree, doctorate degree

University of Wyoming
Department of Renewable Resources
PO Box 3354
Laramie, WY 82071-3354

232

307/766-2263
http://uwadmnweb.uwyo.edu/UWRENEWABLE/
Renewable_Rangeland_Ecology.asp
Degrees available: Bachelor's degree, master's degree, doctorate
degree

Utah State University
Department of Forest, Range, and Wildlife Sciences
5230 Old Main Hill
Logan, UT 84322-5230
435/797-3219
FRWS@cnr.usu.edu
http://www.cnr.usu.edu/front.asp
Degrees available: Bachelor's degree, master's degree, doctorate
degree

For More Information:

Society for Range Management
10030 W 27th Avenue
Wheat Ridge, CO 80215-6601
info@rangelands.org
http://www.rangelands.org

U.S. Department of Agriculture
Natural Resources Conservation Service
PO Box 2890
Washington, DC 20013
http://www.nrcs.usda.gov

U.S. Department of Agriculture
U.S. Forest Service
1400 Independence Avenue, SW
Washington, DC 20250-0003
http://www.fs.fed.us

U.S. Department of the Interior
Bureau of Land Management
1849 C Street, NW, Room 406-LS
Washington, DC 20240
http://www.blm.gov

U.S. Department of the Interior
National Park Service
1849 C Street, NW
Washington, DC 20240
http://www.nps.gov

Recreation Therapy

People don't often stop to consider the link between recreation and health. Studies have proven that both children and older adults enjoy stronger mental and physical capacity and better social interaction if they recreate. Certified recreation therapists use ingenuity and imagination to enhance people's physical, cognitive, and emotional well-being through leisure activities. According to Temple University's Therapeutic Recreation (TR) Program, TR interventions include adapted aquatics, adapted fitness activity, adventure programming, animal assisted therapy, aquatics therapy, creative arts, exercise programs, horticulture, journaling, leisure education, medical play, music, social skills training, stress management, T'ai Chi Chuan, therapeutic horseback riding, wheelchair sports, and Yoga. While all of the listed educational programs focus on using recreation as a therapeutic medium, some programs offer recreation therapy in the department of education as an option in secondary education while other programs focus primarily on a health sciences curriculum and/or a parks and recreation curriculum. Recreation Therapy is sometimes referred to as Therapeutic Recreation.

Typical Courses:

> Introduction to Health Professions
> Contemporary Aspects of Disability
> Professional Seminar
> Research and Evaluation
> Teaching Health Promotion through Leisure Education
> Health Psychology and Human Behavior
> Sport and Recreation for Individuals with Disabilities
> Foundations of Professional Therapeutic Recreation Practice
> TR Assessment and Documentation
> Clinical Procedures in Therapeutic Recreation
> Modalities in Therapeutic Recreation Practice
> Therapeutic Recreation Administration

Potential Employers:

> Hospitals
> Nursing homes
> Adult day programs
> Outpatient centers

> Retirement communities
> Developmental disability centers
> Substance recovery programs
> Schools
> Mental health agencies
> Home health care agencies
> Correctional facilities
> Municipal recreation centers

Available At:

The following list of schools offering programs in therapeutic recreation is not exhaustive. For more programs, visit http://www.recreationtherapy.com/trcollg.htm or http://www.atra-tr.org/curriculumguide.htm.

Arizona State University
School of Community Resources and Development
Agriculture (AG) 281
Tempe, AZ 85287-4703
480/965-7291
http://scrd.asu.edu/undergrad/index.shtml
Degrees available: Bachelor's degree

Eastern Washington University
Department of Physical Education Health and Recreation
200 Physical Education Building
Cheney, WA 99004
509/359-2486
http://www.ewu.edu/x16380.xml
Degrees available: Bachelor's degree

Illinois State University
School of Kinesiology and Recreation
Campus Box 5120
Normal, IL 61790-5120
309/438-8661
kinrec@ilstu.edu
http://www.kinrec.ilstu.edu/undergraduate/info.ther_rec.shtml
Degrees available: Bachelor's degree

Ithaca College
Department of Therapeutic Recreation and Leisure Services
9 Hill Center

Ithaca, NY 14850
607/274-3335
morse@ithaca.edu
http://www.ithaca.edu/admission/programs/programs/tr
Degrees available: Bachelor's degree

Mercy College
Division of Education
555 Broadway
Dobbs Ferry, NY 10522
914/674-7350
http://www.mercy.edu/AcaDivisions/education/TherapRec.cfm
Degrees available: Bachelor's degree

University of North Carolina-Wilmington
Department of Health and Applied Human Sciences
601 South College Road
Wilmington, NC 28403-5956
910/962-3250
kinneyt@uncw.edu
http://www.uncw.edu/hahs/academics-therapeuticrec.htm
Degrees available: Bachelor's degree

Southern University and A&M College
College of Education
Baton Rouge, LA 70813
607/274-3335
http://www.subr.edu/search.htm
Degrees available: Bachelor's degree

Temple University
College of Health Professions
313 Vivacqua Hall
Philadelphia, PA 19122
215/204-6278
http://www.temple.edu/tr/what_is.htm
Degree programs available: Bachelor's degree, master's degree, doctorate degree

Winston-Salem State University
School of Education, Department of Human Performance and Sport Sciences
237 Anderson Center
Winston-Salem, NC 27110-0001
336/750-2370

http://www.wssu.edu/WSSU/UndergraduateStudies/
School+of+Education
Degrees available: Bachelor's degree

University of Wisconsin-La Crosse
Department of Recreation Management and Therapeutic Recreation
1725 State Street, 128 Wittich Hall
La Crosse, WI 54601
608/785-8205
http://www.uwlax.edu/sah/rmtr
Degrees available: Bachelor's degree, master's degree

For More Information:

American Therapeutic Recreation Association
1414 Prince Street, Suite 204
Alexandria, VA 22314
703/683-9420
atra@atra-tr.org
http://www.atra-tr.org

Therapeutic Recreation Directory
http://www.recreationtherapy.com

Interview: Catherine Coyle

Dr. Catherine Coyle is the Undergraduate Coordinator of the Therapeutic Recreation Program at Temple University in Philadelphia, Pennsylvania. She discussed the program and the education of therapeutic recreation students with the editors of *They Teach That in College!?*

Q. Please provide a brief overview of your program.

A. The therapeutic recreation (TR) program at Temple University is a 121-credit, Bachelor of Science degree. It prepares students to become recreation therapists who work collaboratively with doctors, nurses, teachers, psychologists, social workers, occupational therapists, and physical therapists to facilitate health, recovery, and wellness in persons with disabilities or chronic illnesses. While this team of health professionals works collectively to achieve these outcomes, recreation therapists have a unique way of contributing-they use recreation, play, and leisure activities. While their practice may seem 'trivial' to the lay person, it isn't. Recreation therapists do much more than 'play and recreate' with people; they understand the connection between health and recreation, and use this understanding to promote recovery and wellness in persons with disabilities. Recreation therapists realize that children cope better with being hospitalized when given a chance to play; that people recovering from illnesses or adapting to disability adjust and stay healthier longer when they are physically and socially active; and, that older adults maintain a sharper mind and a higher level of social involvement when they recreate.

Did You Know?

According to the U.S. Department of Labor, employment opportunities in therapeutic recreation are promising given the growth of long-term care facilities and physical and psychiatric rehabilitation. It is the 12th fastest growing occupation requiring a bachelor's degree.

At Temple, you will come to learn, understand, and value the unique role of recreation therapists in the health and human service system-to promote play, recreation, and leisure as a means to psychological and physical recovery, health, and well-being among individuals with disabilities, including children, adolescents, adults and older adults. In this curriculum, you will learn how to use counseling techniques, recreation activities, and other activity-based interventions to help individuals with physical, cognitive, emotional or social impairments recover basic motor functioning and reasoning abilities, adapt psychologically, build confidence, socialize effectively, and live fully in their communities.

Because of this, we place a heavy emphasis on assuring that students have a solid foundation in the social and physical sciences, as well as in related areas of health and counseling. The primary goal of any undergraduate TR program is to prepare entry level recreation therapists who can deliver rehabilitation, health promotion, and disease prevention programs to individuals with disabilities across the lifespan and in diverse health and human service settings.

Temple's TR department not only has a distinguished tradition of preparing recreation therapists; it is also uniquely different from other programs throughout the nation. First, Temple is the only university in the nation that has a department dedicated exclusively to the discipline of therapeutic recreation. This means that the instruction and experiences you get are focused solely on preparing you to be a recreation therapist. Secondly, the department is housed within the College of Health Professions; therefore you will interact with future colleagues—students majoring in other disciplines like nursing, occupational therapy, physical therapy, health information management, exercise science, and public health. In fact, recreation therapy students at Temple University have the opportunity to earn a certificate in interdisciplinary studies as a part of their coursework. Additionally, you will be taught not only by nationally recognized scholars and researchers, but by individuals with diverse backgrounds and clinical practice experiences, which means you benefit from our knowledge, professional connections, and commitment to preparing the next generation of leaders. Finally, Philadelphia is an ideal setting for anyone interested in the health professions. Strategically located between Washington, D.C. and New York, it is a large metropolitan area rich in diversity and cultural experiences. You will have easy access to a wealth of varied internship and volunteer opportunities during your academic career. For instance, within the immediate vicinity of Temple University, there are five different, free-standing pediatric hospitals, four free-standing physical rehabilitation hospitals, four free-standing behavioral health hospitals, as well as numerous nursing homes, day programs, schools, and residential facilities that employ recreation therapists. Because of these opportunities, you have numerous venues from which to engage in service-learning activities that will allow you to integrate academic learning with real-life practice. Not only will you complete a set of specific courses in the major; you will also complete two credit-earning, field-based clinical internships that allow you to gain hands-on practical experience as a recreation therapist. Your accumulated experience by graduation is also enhanced by other non-credit earning requirements, including 120 hours of professional development experiences, certification in First-Aid/CPR, and a technology skills competency test.

The Temple TR program is held in high regard nationally and locally. This recognition results directly from the leadership provided by alumni of our program. Alumni have been past presidents of national and local professional organizations as well as recipients of awards and recognitions for their clinical and service activities. They work in a wide range of health and human service agencies locally and nationally demonstrating that Temple 'Owls' are everywhere!

Q. What high school subjects/activities should students focus on to be successful in this major?

A. Students should take college preparatory courses, especially math and science courses. If your school offers psychology or anatomy courses, take them as well because these courses will also be helpful. Being involved in extracurricular activities is also important. Skills developed through your participation in sports, art, music, dance, photography, computers, the debate team, or the community service club are assets you will draw upon as a recreation therapist. If you are adept at foreign languages, continue them. The ability to be bilingual is increasingly important for health care professionals.

Q. What are the most important personal and professional qualities for therapeutic recreation (TR) majors?

A. This major might be a good fit for you if you are interested in a health-related career, enjoy being physically and socially active, have strong leisure pursuits, and have a strong interest in helping others. Because you will routinely use recreation activities in the course of your work, you should have a varied assortment of active and creative leisure pursuits. As a recreation therapist you will be working with children, adolescents, adults, and/or older adults who have a chronic illness or disability; therefore, you should be comfortable interacting with people, and interested in helping others. Additionally, you will often be asked to lead groups of people in activities. Therefore, effective leadership and communication skills are important, as are enthusiasm, creativity, and ingenuity. Finally, students interested in majoring in therapeutic recreation must truly believe that they can "learn more about someone in an hour of play than in a lifetime of conversation" (Plato).

Q. What advice would you offer TR majors as they graduate and look for jobs?

A. First and foremost, I would remind students that through their coursework in TR they have learned much more than what is captured by reading the list of courses on their academic transcript. They have learned to be articulate leaders, to be comfortable interacting with diverse populations, to think creatively, and to see possibilities where none are readily apparent. These skills, as well as the academic content they have mastered, will serve them well! Why? Because, these are skills that employers in diverse settings desire and they are a set of skills that are readily transferable to other careers.

I would also tell graduates that the process of landing your first job begins long before you send out your first resume. Throughout your education, you will be presented with opportunities to become professionally active. Seize them! What will make your resume stand out from others is the extent to which it sets you apart and distinguishes you as an active and committed professional. So, be sure your resume captures your commitment to TR as a profession! Be active and involved as a student. Embrace opportunities to join professional organizations, develop specialized or new skills, and attend conferences. I also encourage students to stay 'connected'. At Temple, many employers forward us employment vacancies well before they post them publicly.

Q. Where do TR graduates find employment?

A. The diversity in employment settings and populations is one of the most exciting things about becoming a recreation therapist. For instance, some recreation therapists choose to work with older adults. They can work with the elderly in intermediate and extended nursing facilities, in adult day centers, or in senior centers. Some prefer to work with children and/or teens.

These individuals might find employment in hospitals, residential facilities, schools or group homes. Others choose to work with adults and can find employment in health care settings (both in-patient and out-patient) or residential facilities. Some enjoy working in mental health settings (hospitals, day treatment centers, group homes, drop-in centers, or correctional facilities). Others find employment opportunities with municipal recreation centers providing support and services for participants with disabilities. Employment opportunities also exist in highly specialized recreation venues, such as therapeutic horseback riding or outdoor adventure activities. Some alumni have even started their own businesses providing recreation assistance to individuals with disabilities residing in the community. According to the U.S. Department of Labor, employment opportunities are expected to continue growing due to expansion in long-term care, physical and psychiatric rehabilitation, and services to people with disabilities in the community.

242

Q. How will the field of therapeutic recreation change in the future?

A. Predicting future change is never easy. However, there are some demographic and health care trends emerging that will provide recreation therapists with new opportunities. The graying of the baby boomers is one such trend. Many of these individuals will retire without giving much thought to how they will fill their retirement time. Accumulating research evidence indicates healthy aging is related to staying active and finding meaning in life after work. Clearly, an emerging role for recreation therapists might be to expand their practice to offer pre- and post-retirement leisure counseling. Another trend is the growing recognition of health promotion and the role of physically and socially active lifestyles in maintaining the health of all individuals, including individuals with disabilities and chronic illnesses. As the only health and human service profession exclusively dedicated to promoting and assuring that individuals with disabilities have the skills and abilities to pursue physically and socially active leisure pursuits, therapeutic recreation professionals have an opportunity to be leaders in designing and delivering health promotion services to persons with disabilities.

Renewable Energy

Energy use in the United States increased by 17 percent between 1991 and 2000, according to the National Energy Policy Development Group. However, our energy production increased by only 2.3 percent. Public concerns about pollution from fossil fuels, increasing costs for conventional energy sources, and our overdependence on foreign energy supplies have created strong interest in renewable energy resources such as wind energy, solar energy, hydropower energy, geothermal energy, and bioenergy. The National Renewable Energy Laboratory estimates that renewable-energy industries will provide at least 300,000 new jobs for American workers over the next two decades. Courses in renewable-energy-related topics can be found at two- and four-year colleges throughout the United States, but only a few institutions offer certificate and degrees in the field.

Typical Courses:

> Physics
> Mathematics
> Introduction to Renewable Energy
> Introduction to Energy Management
> Renewable Energy Applications
> Photovoltaic Theory and System Design
> Photovoltaic Installation
> Electrical Systems
> Introduction to Wind Energy
> Introduction to Solar Energy
> Introduction to Hydropower
> Introduction to Geothermal Energy
> Introduction to Bioenergy

Potential Employers:

> Manufacturing companies
> Research and development companies
> Utility companies
> Government agencies (such as the National Renewable Energy Laboratory and the Energy Efficiency and Renewable Energy Clearinghouse)
> Nonprofit groups and agencies

> Colleges and universities
> Trade associations
> Engineering firms
> Architecture firms

Available At:

The following list of colleges that offer courses and majors in renewable energy and related fields is not exhaustive. Visit http://eereweb.ee.doe.gov/education/higher_education_programs.html or http://www.irecusa.org for more programs.

Bismarck State College
Process Plant Technology Program
1500 Edwards Avenue, PO Box 5587
Bismarck, ND 58506
800/852-5685
http://www.bismarckstate.edu/energy/students/prop
Degrees available: Associate degree

Humboldt State University
Environmental Resources Engineering Program
1 Harpst Street, House 18
Arcata, CA 95521
707/826-3619
ere_dept@humboldt.edu
http://www.humboldt.edu/~ere_dept/academics/energy_descr.html
Degrees available: Bachelor's degree

Iowa State University
Office of Biorenewables Programs
Biorenewable Resources and Technology Program
283 Metals Development Building
Ames, IA 50011-3020
515/294-6555
biomass@iastate.edu
http://www.biorenew.iastate.edu/graduate/degree_options.html
Degrees available: Master's degree, doctorate degree

Lane Community College
Science Department
Renewable Energy Technician Program Option
4000 East 30th Avenue, Building 16, Room 253
541/463-3977
ebbager@lanecc.edu

Eugene, OR 97405
http://lanecc.edu/instadv/catalog/science/programs/energy.htm
Degrees available: Associate degree

Minnesota West Community and Technical College
Renewable Energy Technology Program
1593 11th Avenue
Granite Falls, MN 56241
800/657-3247
http://www.mnwest.edu/academics/programs/manu/rnewaas.htm
Degrees available: Associate degree

Oregon Institute of Technology
3201 Campus Drive
Klamath Falls, OR 97601
541/885-1000
http://www.oit.edu
Degrees available: Bachelor's degree

San Juan College
Renewable Energy Program
4601 College Boulevard
Farmington, NM 87402
505/326-3311
http://www.sanjuancollege.edu/academics/technology/RENG
Degrees available: Certificate, associate degree

Sonoma State University
Department of Environmental Studies and Planning
Energy Management and Design Program
1801 East Cotati Avenue
Rohnert Park, CA 94928
707/664-2430
http://www.sonoma.edu/ensp/academic_plan_energy.htm
Degrees available: Bachelor's degree

For More Information:

American Solar Energy Society
2400 Central Avenue, Suite A
Boulder, CO 80301
303/443-3130
ases@ases.org
http://www.ases.org

American Wind Energy Association
1101 14th Street, NW, 12th Floor

Washington, DC 20005
202/383-2500
windmail@awea.org
http://www.awea.org

Association of Energy Engineers
4025 Pleasantdale Road, Suite 420
Atlanta, GA 30340
http://www.aeecenter.org

Geothermal Education Office
664 Hilary Drive
Tiburon, CA 94920
415/435-4574
geo@marin.org
http://www.geothermal.marin.org

Geothermal Energy Association
209 Pennsylvania Avenue, SE
Washington, DC 20003
202/454-5261
research@geo-energy.org
http://www.geo-energy.org

Interstate Renewable Energy Council
POB 1156
Latham, NY 12110-1156
518/458-6059
info@irecusa.org
http://www.irecusa.org

Midwest Renewable Energy Association
7558 Deer Road
Custer, WI 54423
715/592-6595
info@the-mrea.org
http://www.the-mrea.org

National Hydropower Association
1 Massachusetts Avenue, NW, Suite 850
Washington, DC 20001
202/682-1700
help@hydro.org
http://www.hydro.org

National Renewable Energy Laboratory
1617 Cole Boulevard
Golden, CO 80401-3393
303/275-3000
http://www.nrel.gov

Renewable Fuels Association
1 Massachusetts Avenue, NW, Suite 820
Washington, DC 20001
202/289-3835
info@ethanolrfa.org
http://www.ethanolrfa.org

Solar Energy Industries Association
805 15th Street, NW, Suite 510
Washington, DC 20005
202/628-7779
info@seia.org
http://www.seia.org

U.S. Department of Energy
Energy Efficiency and Renewable Energy
http://www.eren.doe.gov and http://eereweb.ee.doe.gov/education/careers_renewable_energy.html

Interview: Tom Munson and Carl Bickford

San Juan College in Farmington, New Mexico, was the first
community college in the United States to offer an associate
degree in renewable energy. The editors of *They Teach That in
College!?* discussed renewable energy and the education of
renewable energy students with Tom Munson, Coordinator of
the College's Renewable Energy program, and Carl Bickford,
Associate Professor of Engineering and one of the founders of
the program, about this interesting academic field.

Q. Tell us about the renewable energy program at San
Juan College.

A. The renewable energy program at San Juan College gives the
student a solid foundation in the science and in the
design/installation techniques required to work with renewable energy technologies. We offer Photovoltaic System

Design and Installation either as an Associate of Applied Science (AAS) degree or as a One-Year Certificate. The certificate is designed for students who already have a college degree, or who currently work in a related industry. Students gain the knowledge and skills necessary to design and safely install electrical energy systems based on current photovoltaic and power conditioning equipment. The curriculum includes hands-on electrical training both in a computer-based laboratory and outdoors doing projects and installations. Training in and compliance with the National Electrical Code is emphasized both in the classroom and during installation practice. For additional information please visit our website at http://www.sanjuancollege.edu/reng.

Q. What types of students enter your program? What are their career goals and interests?

A. The students who enter the program are looking for a career change and want to make a positive difference in the world. They often want to translate academic knowledge into real-world physical projects.

Q. What type of career path does the average student take upon graduating from your program?

A. Most students end up working in the PV (photovoltaic) industry in varying capacities. Some get jobs working as designers and installers for solar companies that do installation and repair services. Others get jobs working for distributors both in technical support capacities and in sales positions. A few have started their own businesses.

Q. What personal qualities do students need to be successful in your program and in their post-college careers?

A. A concern about the environment, wanting to make a difference, and a desire to make this world a better place to live in are qualities that will help students to be successful in the program.

Basic science and math skills and basic tool skills will be helpful in completing the program. Although it isn't required, skill in working with one's hands and prior electrical knowledge and wiring experience are also beneficial.

Q. What is the future for your program and renewable energy?

A. Our program will grow along with the renewable energy industry, which continues to grow in both this country and the world at large. This an industry that will be on the leading edge as the consciousness of the society increases.

Screenwriting

If you've ever dreamed of winning an Academy Award, and you have a talent for writing, a major in screenwriting might help you develop your skills and give you the background and contacts in the film industry to get your career started. Or maybe your interests lie in writing for television. In television screenwriting programs, you can learn to develop scripts for dramatic forms ranging from action-adventure, to social drama, to situational comedy. No matter your interests you will learn about the elements of character, dialogue, scene, setting, texture, style, and tone via intensive workshop classes. Writing scenes, short scripts, treatments, and finally full-length feature screenplays—ready to be pitched to agents—is what a student majoring in screenwriting can expect. A combination of creative talent, storytelling ability, and college study (associate, bachelor's, and master's degrees are available in screenwriting), will give you a leg up over others in this highly competitive industry.

Typical Courses:

> Dramatic Structure
> Editing
> Visual Storytelling
> Film and Television Aesthetics
> Introduction to Screenwriting
> History of Film and Television
> Acting for Non-Actors
> Seminar in Television and Film Writing
> Narrative Theory and Practice for Screenwriters
> Writing Screenplay Adaptations
> Film and Television Genres

Potential Employers:

> Movie studios
> Self-employment (freelance writer)
> Production companies
> Talent agencies
> Advertising agencies

Available At:

The University of the Arts
320 South Broad Street
Philadelphia, PA 19102
800/616-ARTS, 215/717-6569
http://www.uarts.edu/ug/mc/wftv/index.cfm
Degrees available: Bachelor's degree

University of California-Los Angeles
School of Theatre, Film, and Television
102 East Melnitz Hall, PO Box 951622
Los Angeles, CA 90095-1622
310/825-5761
info@tft.ucla.edu
http://www.tft.ucla.edu/ftv_mfa/index.cfm?action=screen
Degrees available: Bachelor's degree (general, with an emphasis in screenwriting), master's degree

Chapman University
Dodge College of Film and Media Arts
One University Drive
DeMille Hall, Room 127
Orange, CA 92866
714/997-6765
DodgeCollege@chapman.edu
http://ftv.chapman.edu/prospective/undergraduate/
screenwriting.cfm
Degrees available: Bachelor's degree

Columbia College Chicago
600 South Michigan Avenue
Chicago, IL 60605-1996
312/663-1600
http://www.colum.edu/undergraduate/filmvideo/screenwriting/sc
reenwritconcreqs.html
Degrees available: Bachelor's degree

Columbia University
School of the Arts
513 Dodge Hall
212/854-2815
film@columbia.edu
http://www.app.cc.columbia.edu/art/app/arts/film/viewProgram.jsp
Degrees available: Master's degree

Did You Know?

The American Screenwriters Association offers the High School Screenwriting Initiative, a one-day seminar for high school students interested in screenwriting. Visit http://www.goasa.com for more information.

Hollins University
Graduate Studies Office
Roanoke, VA 24020
540/362-6575
hugrad@hollins.edu
http://www.hollins.edu/grad/film/screenwriting.htm
Degrees available: Master's degree

Metropolitan State University
Communication, Writing, and the Arts Department
700 Seventh Street E
St. Paul, MN 55106-5000
651/793-1212
http://www.metrostate.edu/catalog/dep_com.html#screen
Degrees available: Bachelor's degree

Minneapolis Community & Technical College
1501 Hennepin Avenue
Minneapolis, MN 55403
612/659-6000
http://www.minneapolis.edu/screenwriting
Degrees available: Associate degree

New York University
Department of Dramatic Writing
721 Broadway, 7th Floor
New York, NY 10003
212/998-1940
rew3@nyu.edu
http://ddw.tisch.nyu.edu/page/undergraduate.html
Degrees available: Bachelor's degree, master's degree

University of Southern California
Writing for Screen and Television Program
University Park, LUC 301
Los Angeles, CA 90089-2211

213/740-3303
writing@cinema.usc.edu
http://www-cntv.usc.edu/academic_programs/writing/
academic-writing-home.cfm
Degrees available: Bachelor's degree, master's degree

For More Information:

American Screenwriters Association
269 South Beverly Drive, Suite 2600
Beverly Hills, CA 90212-3807
866/265-9091
asa@goasa.com
http://www.asascreenwriters.com

Sundance Institute
8530 Wilshire Boulevard, 3rd Floor
Beverly Hills, CA 90211-3114
310/360-1981
la@sundance.org
http://www.sundance.org

253

Writers Guild of America
East Chapter
555 West 57th Street, Suite 1230
New York, NY 10019
212/767-7800
http://www.wgaeast.org

Writers Guild of America
West Chapter
7000 West Third Street
Los Angeles, CA 90048
800/548-4532
http://www.wga.org

Screenwriter's Utopia
http://www.screenwritersutopia.com

Ski Resort Management

Combine your passion with snow sports with a top-notch college education! Ski resort managers are employed at mountain operations and resorts throughout the United States in positions such as resort director, ski instructor, and equipment and operations manager. In postsecondary ski management programs, technical and academic instruction is provided, coupled with practical experience in the form of an internship or fieldwork. Degree choices range from a certification course to a bachelor's degree.

Typical Courses:

> Resort Budgeting and Organization
> Resort Master Planning
> Resort Merchandising
> Resort Mountain Operations
> Snow Science
> Ski Business Management
> Methods for the Professional Ski Teacher
> Ski Lift Construction and Design
> Ski Equipment Mechanics
> Internship in Ski Business and Resort Management

Potential Employers:

> Ski Resorts

Available At:

Gogebic Community College
E- 4946 Jackson Road
Ironwood, MI 49938
906/932-4231, ext. 269
http://www.gogebic.cc.mi.us/departments/sam_div
Degrees available: Associate degree (Transferable courses to Northern Michigan University's bachelor's program in ski business management)

Lyndon State College
Recreation Resource and Ski Resort Management
1001 College Road
Lyndonville, VT 05851

802/626-6200
http://www.lyndonstate.edu/rec/main/index.php?body=programs
Degrees available: Bachelor's degree

University of Maine-Farmington
Ski Industries Certificate Program
228 Main Street
Farmington, ME 04938
ebreiden@maine.edu
http://www.umf.maine.edu/~ski
Degrees available: Certificate program (must be combined with
a bachelor's degree in any discipline)

Northern Michigan University
College of Business
1401 Presque Isle Avenue
Marquette, MI 49855
http://www.nmu.edu/business/skimgt.htm
Degrees available: Bachelor's degree (Joint program with
Gogebic Community College. Some courses must be taken at
Gogebic Community College.)

Sierra Nevada College
Department of Management
Incline Village, NV 89451
http://www.sierranevada.edu/academic/business/mm.htm#skibusiness
Degrees available: Bachelor's degree

Western State College of Colorado
Department of Recreation
Gym 209
Gunnison, CO 81231
http://www.western.edu/recreation/program.html
Degrees available: Bachelor's degree

For More Information:

National Ski Areas Association
133 South Van Gordon Street, Suite 300
Lakewood, CO 80228
nsaa@nsaa.org
http://www.nsaa.org

Professional Ski Instructors of America
133 South Van Gordon Street, Suite 101
Lakewood, CO 80228
http://www.psia.org

Southwest Studies

The American Southwest is a lively medley of cultures, ethnic groups, traditions, and history. Southwest Studies examines the greater Southwest (Arizona, Colorado, New Mexico, and Utah—some schools also include portions of California and Texas in this group) from anthropological, archeological, artistic, cultural, ethnographic, historical, linguistic, political, and other perspectives. In addition to interdisciplinary study, one of the most exciting aspects of Southwest studies classes are the extensive field trips that most classes take, exploring ancient, but still occupied, Pueblo villages along the Rio Grande River in New Mexico; Anasazi ruins in Arizona, New Mexico, Utah, and Colorado; and multicultural meccas such as Santa Fe, New Mexico. Degrees in Southwest studies are available at all academic levels.

Typical Courses:

256

> Southwestern Arts and Culture
> History of the Southwest
> Topics in Anthropology
> Native Peoples of the Southwest
> Contemporary Hispanic Writers of the Southwest
> Sustainable Development
> Social and Cultural Dynamics of the Southwest
> Chicano Studies
> Archaeology of the Borderlands
> Environmental Justice

Potential Employers:

> Colleges and universities
> Secondary schools
> Government agencies
> Research-oriented organizations
> Museums and cultural centers

Available At:

Colorado College
The Hulbert Center for Southwestern Studies
14 East Cache la Poudre
Colorado Springs, CO 80903

719/389-6647
http://www.coloradocollege.edu/dept/SW/swstudies/
majminorswstudies.htm
Degrees available: Bachelor's degree

Fort Lewis College
Department of Southwest Studies
1000 Rim Drive
Durango, CO 81301-3999
970/247-7010
http://www.fortlewis.edu/academics/programs/
southwest_studies.asp
Degrees available: Bachelor's degree

New Mexico Highlands University
Department of Anthropology
3343 Hewett Hall, PO Box 9000
Las Vegas, NM 87701
505/454-3554, 877/850-9064
http://www.nmhu.edu/anthropology/masouthwest.php
Degrees available: Master's degree

University of New Mexico-Los Alamos
4000 University Drive
Los Alamos, NM 87554
505/662-0332, 800/894-5919
stuserv@la.unm.edu
http://www.la.unm.edu/admissions/degrees_certificates.html
Degrees available: Certificate, associate degree

Southern Methodist University
William P. Clements Center for Southwest Studies
William P. Clements Department of History
PO Box 750176
Dallas, TX 75275-0176
214/768-2984
hist@mail.smu.edu
http://www.smu.edu/history/phd.asp or
http://www.smu.edu/swcenter
Degrees available: Doctorate degree

For More Information:

American Association of Museums
1575 Eye Street, NW, Suite 400
Washington, DC 20005
http://www.aam-us.org

Speech Pathology

Speech pathologists work to diagnose and treat speech and language disorders, as well as swallowing disorders. They work with children and adults whose speech is compromised due to physical or neurological disorders, developmental delays, or injury. Many speech pathologists also work with geriatric clients whose language and speech is affected due to sickness, such as a stroke. In fact, according to the *Occupational Outlook Handbook,* the biggest demand for speech pathologists will be from the growing elderly population who will need services to help adjust to chronic illness. The minimum educational requirement to work in this profession is a master's degree.

Typical Courses:

> Clinical Methods
> Organic Disorders
> Communication Problems of the Aged
> Evaluation and Treatment of Dysphagia in Adults
> Augmentative Communication
> Motor Speech Disorders and Cerebral Palsy
> Developmental Speech Disorders
> Acquired Speech and Language Disorders
> Articulation Disorders
> Stuttering
> Evaluation of Children

Potential Employers:

> Schools
> Health maintenance organizations
> Hospitals
> Public health departments
> Research agencies
> Colleges and universities
> Private practice
> Long-term care facilities
> Rehabilitation centers
> Government agencies
> Industrial audiology
> Corporate speech-language pathology programs

Available At:

The following list offers a selection of schools that award degrees in speech pathology. For a complete listing, visit the American Speech-Language-Hearing Association's website at http://www.asha.org/gradguide.

Arizona State University
Department of Speech and Hearing Science
PO Box 870102
Tempe, AZ 85287-0102
480/965-2374
shsgrad@asu.edu
http://www.asu.edu/clas/shs
Degrees available: Bachelor's degree, master's degree, doctorate degree

Did You Know?

The U.S. Department of Labor predicts that the field of speech-language pathology will grow faster than the average for all occupations through 2012.

California State University-Fresno
Department of Communicative Sciences and Disorders
5048 North Jackson Avenue, M/S LS80
Fresno, CA 93740-8022
559/278-2423
donfr@csufresno.edu
http://www.csufresno.edu/csd
Degrees available:: Bachelor's degree, master's degree

University of Colorado-Boulder
Department of Speech, Language, and Hearing Sciences
2501 Kittredge Loop Road, 409 UCB
Boulder, CO 80309-0409
303/492-6445
slhsgrad@colorado.edu
http://www.colorado.edu/slhs
Degree programs available: Bachelor's degree, master's degree, doctorate degree

University of Florida
Department of Communication Sciences and Disorders
336 Dauer Hall, PO Box 117420
Gainesville, FL 32611-7420
352/392-2113
http://web.csd.ufl.edu
Degrees available: Bachelor's degree, master's degree, doctorate degree

University of Georgia
Department of Communication Sciences and Special Education
516 Aderhold Hall
Athens, GA 30602-7153
706/542-4561
csd@uga.edu
http://www.coe.uga.edu/csse
Degrees available: Bachelor's degree, master's degree, doctorate degree

260

Howard University
Department of Communication Sciences and Disorders
525 Bryant Street, NW
John H. Johnson Building
Washington, DC 20059
202/806-6990
oharris@howard.edu
www.howard.edu/schoolcommunications/CSD/About.htm
Degrees available: Bachelor's degree, master's degree

University of Illinois-Urbana-Champaign
Department of Speech and Hearing Science
901 South 6th Street, 220 Speech and Hearing Science Building
Champaign, IL 61820
217/333-2230
shs@uiuc.edu
http://www.shs.uiuc.edu
Degrees available: Bachelor's degree, master's degree, doctorate degree

University of Kansas
Intercampus Program in Communicative Disorders
Department of Speech, Language, Hearing Sciences and Disorders
3901 Rainbow Boulevard
Kansas City, KS 66160-7605
913/588-5937
jferraro@kumc.edu

http://www.ku.edu/~splh/ipcd
Degrees available: Bachelor's degree, master's degree, doctorate degree

University of Louisville
Surgery/Graduate Program in Communicative Disorders
Health Sciences Center, Myers Hall
Louisville, KY 40292
502/852-5274
http://www.louisville.edu/medschool/surgery/com-disorders
Degrees available: Master's degree

University of Maine-Orono
Department Of Communication Sciences and Disorders
5724 Dunn Hall
Orono, ME 04469-5724
207/581-2006
mboyd@maine.edu
http://www.umaine.edu/comscidis
Degrees available: Bachelor's degree, master's degree

University of Massachusetts-Amherst
Department of Communication Disorders
715 North Pleasant Street
Amherst, MA 01003-9304
413/545-0131
proginfo@comdis.umass.edu
http://www.umass.edu/sphhs/comdis
Degrees available: Bachelor's degree, master's degree, doctorate degree

University of Minnesota
Speech-Language-Hearing Sciences
164 Pillsbury Drive, SE, 115 Shevlin Hall
Minneapolis, MN 55455
612/624-3322
slhs@unm.edu
http://www.slhs.umn.edu
Degrees available: Bachelor's degree, master's degree, doctorate degree

University of Oregon
Communication Disorders and Sciences Program
5284 University of Oregon
Eugene, OR 97403-5284
541/346-2480

Did You Know?

Speech-language pathologists who were certified by the American Speech-Language-Hearing Association had median annual salaries that ranged from $45,000 to $52,600 in 2003.

robertsk@uoregon.edu
http://education.uoregon.edu/cds
Degrees available: Bachelor's degree, master's degree, doctorate degree

University of North Texas
Department of Speech and Hearing Sciences
PO Box 305010
Denton, TX 76203-5010
940/565-2481
ritag@unt.edu
http://www.sphs.unt.edu
Degrees available: Bachelor's degree, master's degree, doctorate degree

University of Southern Mississippi
Department of Speech and Hearing Sciences
118 College Drive, #5092
Hattiesburg, MS 39406-0001
601/266-5216
shs@usm.edu
http://www.usm.edu/shs
Degrees available: Bachelor's degree, master's degree, doctorate degree

Western Michigan University
Department of Speech Pathology and Audiology
Kalamazoo, MI 49008-5355
616/387-8045
http://www.wmich.edu/hhs/sppa
Degrees available: Bachelor's degree, master's degree, doctorate degree

University of Wyoming
Division of Communication Disorders
1000 East University Avenue, PO Box 3311
Laramie, WY 82071

307/766-6427
woodall@uwyo.edu
http://www.uwyo.edu/comdis
Degrees available: Bachelor's degree, master's degree

For More Information:

American Speech-Language-Hearing Association
10801 Rockville Pike
Rockville, MD 20852
actioncenter@asha.org
http://www.asha.org

National Student Speech Language Hearing Association
10801 Rockville Pike
Rockville, MD 20852
800/498-2071
nsslha@asha.org
http://www.nsslha.org

Interview: Sid P. Bacon

Dr. Sid P. Bacon is the Chairman of the Department of Speech and Hearing Science at Arizona State University in Tempe, Arizona. He discussed his program and the education of speech pathology students with the editors of *They Teach That in College!?*

Q. Please provide a brief overview of your program.

A. Arizona State University offers a bachelor of science degree in speech and hearing Science. It focuses on the scientific aspects of normal speech, language, and hearing, and includes a few courses on various disorders of human communication. Our students are very well prepared to pursue graduate training in either speech-language pathology or audiology. Graduate degrees are generally necessary to practice clinically. [Note: The University also offers a master of science degree in communication disorders (with an emphasis in speech-language pathology), an Au.D. degree (Doctorate of Audiology), and a Ph.D. degree (Doctorate of Philosophy).]

Q. What high school subjects/activities should students focus on to be successful in this major?

A. Students would benefit from courses in biology, psychology, child development, physics, and mathematics. They also would benefit from extracurricular activities such as baby-sitting, working in physician's offices or nursing homes, and participating in activities with individuals with special needs.

Q. How will the field of speech language pathology change in the future?

A. Advances in science and technology in areas such as brain imaging and genetics will lead to a better understanding of the causes of communication disorders and consequently to better treatments. There is likely to be a greater emphasis on communication at both ends of the age spectrum. On the young end, there will be a growing emphasis on early intervention as it pertains to language and literacy—getting children ready to read and be successful in school. At the older end, there will be a greater emphasis on how to improve communication and avoid or minimize the social isolation that often accompanies the decline in communication abilities in the elderly. The field also will continue to expand to help address communication problems globally, particularly in third-world countries.

Sports Media

Sports media is a field experiencing explosive growth due the public's seemingly unquenchable interest in sports and increasing coverage on cable television and the Internet. Programs in sports media blend liberal arts and specialized courses to provide a thorough examination of the economic, cultural, historical, and ethical aspects of sport. Graduates will find work as media planners, producers, sports information directors, sports journalists, and specialists in public relations and promotion.

Typical Courses:

> Sport video production
> Sport marketing
> Public relations
> Advertising
> Field work in sport management and media
> Promotion management
> Sport internet marketing
> Sport governance
> Media writing
> Social aspects of sport

Potential Employers:

> Commissioners' and league offices
> Major and minor league professional sports teams
> Amateur leagues
> Colleges and universities
> Foundations and conferences
> Media organizations
> Sports marketing firms
> Sports arenas
> Newspapers and magazines
> Radio stations
> Television stations

Available At:

Ithaca College
Department of Sport Management and Media
12 Hill Center
Ithaca, NY 14850
607/274-3192
http://www.ithaca.edu/admission/programs/programs/sic
Degree available: Bachelor's degree

For More Information:

Broadcast Education Association
1771 N Street, NW
Washington, DC 20036-2891
202/429-5355
beainfo@beaweb.org
http://www.beaweb.org

National Association of Broadcasters
1771 N Street, NW
Washington, DC 20036-2891
202/429-5300
nab@nab.org
http://www.nab.org

National Association for Sport and Physical Education
1900 Association Drive
Reston, VA 20191-1598
800/213-7193, ext. 410
naspe@aahperd.org
http://www.aahperd.org/naspe/template.cfm

Sports Ministry

Sports ministry is a unique approach to sharing the message of Jesus Christ with people everywhere, allowing students to channel their God-given athletic talents and abilities into being effective ministers. The commonality of sports and recreation across so many age groups, institutions, and cultures makes athletic activity an excellent avenue for sharing the word of the Lord and modeling Christian values and experiences, both on and off of the field. Students who enroll in a sports ministry program can expect to study general academics; religious-themed subjects such as the Bible, evangelism, and ministerial skills; and sports-related subjects such as coaching, fitness and wellness, and the mechanics of sports games. A sports ministry program prepares students to work together with athletes, missionaries, churches, and others to spread the Christian message in many different, often multicultural, environments, at home or abroad. For example, some sports ministers work in prisons, schools, churches, community organizations, and international missions.

Typical Courses:

> Christian Theology
> Models of Christian Ministry
> Old Testament/New Testament
> Communicating the Christian Faith
> Theological Foundations for Sports Ministry
> Administration and Organization of Sports Ministry
> Evangelism and Discipleship in Sports Ministry
> Leadership and Staff Dynamics

Potential Employers:

> Nonprofit religious organizations
> Camp ministries
> Churches

Available At:

Crossroads College
920 Mayowood Road, SW
Rochester, MN 55902
507/288-4563

http://www.crossroadscollege.edu/Academic_Programs/
sports_ministry_major.htm
Degrees available: Bachelor's degree

Huntington University
Department of Recreation
2303 College Avenue
Huntington, IN 46750
260/356-6000
http://www.huntington.edu/rec/sportsministry.htm
Degrees available: Bachelor's degree

Malone College
School of Theology
515 25th Street, NW
Canton, OH 44709
800/521-1146
http://www.malone.edu/2202
Degrees available: Bachelor's degree

Moody Bible Institute
820 North LaSalle Boulevard
Chicago IL, 60610
312/329-4000
http://mmm.moody.edu/GenMoody/
default.asp?sectionID=BB135E240ED24EEC99617246CE147E84
Degrees available: Bachelor's degree

Washington Bible College
6511 Princess Garden Parkway
Lanham, MD 20706
301/552-1400
http://true441.youthsite.org/
index.cfm?PAGE_ID=330&EXPAND=319
Degrees available: Bachelor's degree

For More Information:

Athletes in Action
651 Taylor Drive
Xenia, OH 45385
937/352-1000
athletesinaction@aia.com
http://www.athletesinaction.org

National Association for Sport and Physical Education
1900 Association Drive

Reston, VA 20191-1598
800/213-7193, ext. 410
naspe@aahperd.org
http://www.aahperd.org/naspe/template.cfm

National Council of Churches USA
475 Riverside Drive, Room 880
New York, NY 10115
212/870-2227
http://ncccusa.org

National Religious Vocation Conference
5420 South Cornell Avenue, Suite 105
Chicago, IL 60615-5604
773/363-5454
NRVC@aol.com
http://www.nrvc.net

Sports Studies

Life-long opportunities for individuals to play sports, on an amateur level, exist in every community. People join teams and leagues for the social and physical benefits they provide. For some people, however, sport is more than just a weekly commitment to your local team—it's a career. If you played football, basketball, volleyball, tennis, soccer, or another sport in high school, and you just can't imagine a life without sports, a career in sports management might be a winning choice for you. Such a program prepares you for a career in sports administration, which could lead to managing or coaching local sporting leagues, developing programming for a parks and recreation department, or marketing your favorite professional team. Students should be aware that some programs place a greater emphasis on the health/physiology of sport while others focus primarily on the business of sports administration. Degrees in this exciting field are available at all academic levels.

270

Typical Courses:

> History of Sports
> Social Aspects of Sports
> Sports Economics
> Sports Marketing
> Legal and Ethical Issues in Sports
> Sports Administration
> Evolution of the Sport Media
> Sports and Exercise Psychology
> Social and Cultural Aspects of Play
> Gender Issues in Sports
> Sports Management and Media

Potential Employers:

> Professional and amateur sports teams and leagues
> Fitness centers
> Recreational sports programs
> Colleges and universities
> Radio and television networks
> Print publications
> Internet companies

Available At:

This list of schools offering programs in sports studies is not exhaustive. For more programs, contact the Sport Management Program Review Council of the National Association of Sport and Physical Education (http://www.aahperd.org/naspe). The North American Society for Sport Management offers undergraduate and graduate directories of sport management programs for a fee. Visit the Society's website, http://www.nassm.com/index.html, for more information.

Bowling Green State University
Sport Management, Recreation, and Tourism Division
Bowling Green, OH 43403-0001
419/372-2531
http://www.bgsu.edu/colleges/edhd/hmsls/smrt/smd
Degrees available: Bachelor's degree

Cardinal Stritch University
Department of Business and Economics
6801 North Yates Road
Milwaukee, WI 53217
414/410-4173
http://www.stritch.edu
Degrees available: Bachelor's degree

Central Michigan University
The Herbert H. and Grace A. Dow College of Health Professions
Mount Pleasant, MI 48859
989/774-1730
chpadmit@cmich.edu
http://www.chp.cmich.edu/pes/sa
Degrees available: Master's degree

Grace College
Physical Education and Sport Studies Department
Winona Lake, IN 46590
574/372-5100, ext. 6263
http://www.grace.edu/grace/undergraduate/catalog/documents/
physical_education.pdf
Degrees available: Bachelor's degree

University of Iowa
Department of Health and Sport Studies
240 Schaeffer Hall
Iowa City, IA 52242-1409

http://www.uiowa.edu/~hss/index.html
Degrees available: Bachelor's degree, master's degree, doctorate
degree

Ithaca College
Department of Sport Management and Media
12 Hill Center
Ithaca, NY 14850
607/274-3192
http://www.ithaca.edu/admission/programs/programs/sm
Degrees available: Bachelor's degree

University of Massachusetts-Amherst
Department of Sport Management
121 Presidents Drive
Amherst, MA 01003
http://www.isenberg.umass.edu/sportmgt
Degrees available: Bachelor's degree, master's degree

New York University
Preston Robert Tisch Center for Hospitality, Tourism, and Sports
Management
145 4th Avenue
New York, NY 10003
http://www.scps.nyu.edu/departments/department.jsp?deptId=23
Degrees available: Bachelor's degree, master's degree

College of St. Joseph
Division of Business
Sports Management Program
71 Clement Road
Rutland, VT 05701
877/270-9998
http://www.csj.edu/acad-business.html
Degrees available: Bachelor's degree

For More Information:

National Association for Sport and Physical Education
1900 Association Drive
Reston, VA 20191-1598
800/213-7193, ext. 410
naspe@aahperd.org
http://www.aahperd.org/naspe/template.cfm

Strategic Intelligence

Intelligence professionals gather information about domestic groups and foreign governments in order to safeguard the security and the interests of the United States and its citizens. This information might be economic, political, or military in nature, or it may focus on threats of terrorism or other criminal activities. The Joint Military Intelligence College, which is attached to the Defense Intelligence Agency, offers the only accredited academic programs in strategic intelligence in the United States. These programs train those interested in obtaining senior positions in the U.S. armed forces and the national security structure. All students must be U.S. citizens who are members of the U.S. armed forces or federal government employees, be nominated by their parent organization, and possess a Top Secret, Sensitive Compartmented Information security clearance prior to enrollment.

Potential Employers:

> U.S. armed forces
> Government agencies (such as the Central Intelligence Agency, the Defense Intelligence Agency, the Federal Bureau of Investigation, and the Department of Homeland Security)

Available At:

Joint Military Intelligence College (JMIC)
JMIC Admissions Office (MCA-2)
200 MacDill Boulevard
Washington, DC 20340-5100
202/231-3299
JMIC@dia.mil
http://www.dia.mil/college/academics.htm
Degrees available: Certificate, bachelor's degree, master's degree, postgraduate certificate

For More Information:

Association of Former Intelligence Officers
6723 Whittier Avenue, Suite 303A
McLean, VA 22101-4533
703/790-0320
afio@afio.com
http://www.afio.com

Did You Know?

Intelligence officers with bachelor's degrees earned starting salaries that ranged from $30,567 to $45,239 in 2005, according to the U.S. Department of Labor.

Central Intelligence Agency
http://www.cia.gov/employment

Defense Intelligence Agency
http://www.dia.mil/employment

Federal Bureau of Investigation
http://www.fbi.gov

U.S. Department of Homeland Security
http://www.dhs.gov

Supply Chain Management

Supply chain management professionals are key players in manufacturing and service industries. According to the Institute for Supply Management, they use their knowledge of purchasing/procurement, transportation/logistics, contract development, negotiation, inventory control, distribution and warehousing, product development, economic forecasting, risk management, and global business to help their companies stay competitive in a global economy. A growing number of colleges and universities are offering degrees in supply chain management (sometimes called logistics and transportation management, global logistics management, operations and supply chain management, transportation and logistics management, and acquisitions management) at the certificate through graduate levels. Other schools offer study in the field via supply chain management concentrations that are part of degrees in business, business administration, business information systems, management, marketing, or other fields.

Typical Classes:

> Introduction to Supply Chain Management
> Economics
> Transportation Management
> Strategic Warehouse Management
> Sales
> Negotiations: Theory and Practice
> Information Technology Tools
> Forecasting in the Supply Chain
> Quality Process Management
> Supply Chain Research and Analysis Techniques
> Inventory Strategies
> E-Commerce and the Supply Chain
> Customer Relationships

Potential Employers:

> Technology companies
> Manufacturing companies
> Service organizations
> Consulting firms
> Any organization that offers products or services

Available At:

The following list of schools offering programs in supply chain management is not exhaustive. For more programs, visit the following website, http://www.ism.ws/ISMMembership/SchoolsOfferingCourses.cfm.

University of Alaska-Anchorage
College of Business and Public Policy
3211 Providence Drive
Anchorage, AK 99508
907/786-4100
http://www.scob.alaska.edu/logistics.asp
Degrees available: Certificate, associate degree, bachelor's degree

Did You Know?

U.S. News & World Report recently selected supply chain management as a hot track career field.

Elmhurst College
Center for Business and Economics
190 Prospect Avenue
Elmhurst, IL 60126-3296
630/617-3500
http://public.elmhurst.edu/business/1275622.html and
http://public.elmhurst.edu/scm
Degrees available: Bachelor's degree, master's degree

Georgia Southern University
Department of Management, Marketing, and Logistics
PO Box 8154
Statesboro, GA 30460
912/681-5655
m_and_m@georgiasouthern.edu
http://coba.georgiasouthern.edu/depts/mml
Degrees available: Bachelor's degree

University of Houston
College of Technology
300 Technology Building
Houston, TX 77204-4021
713/743-4100

wakudrle@uh.edu
http://www.tech.uh.edu/departments/ilt/ilt_index.htm
Degrees available: Bachelor's degree, master's degree

Iowa State University
Department of Logistics, Operations, and Management
Information Systems
1320 Gerdin Business Building
Ames, IA 50011-2065
515/294-3659
undergrad@iastate.edu
http://www.bus.iastate.edu/OSCM
Degrees available: Bachelor's degree

Michigan State University
Eli Broad College of Business
East Lansing, MI 48824
517/355-8377
webhelp@bus.msu.edu
http://www.bus.msu.edu
Degrees available: Bachelor's degree, master's degree, doctorate
degree

Northwestern University
The Transportation Center
600 Foster Street
Evanston, IL 60208-4055
847/491-7287
http://transportation.northwestern.edu
Degrees available: Undergraduate minor, master's degree

The Ohio State University
Department of Marketing and Logistics
2100 Neil Avenue, Fisher Hall, Suite 500
Columbus, OH 43210-1144
614/292-9695
http://fisher.osu.edu/departments/marketing/academic-programs
Degrees available: Bachelor's degree, master's degree, doctorate
degree

Syracuse University
Mary J. Whitman School of Management
721 University Avenue
Syracuse, NY 13244-2450
315/443-3751
stwebste@syr.edu

http://whitman.syr.edu/supplychain
Degrees available: Bachelor's degree, master's degree, doctorate degree

Weber State University
Department of Business Administration
3850 University Circle
Ogden, UT 84408
801/626-6063
gsbe@weber.edu
http://goddard.weber.edu
Degrees available: Bachelor's degree

For More Information:

American Society of Transportation and Logistics
1700 North Moore Street, Suite 1900
Arlington, VA 22209
703/524-5011
astl@nitl.org
http://www.astl.org

Council of Supply Chain Management Professionals
2805 Butterfield Road, Suite 200
Oak Brook, IL 60523-1170
630/574-0985
cscmpadmin@cscmp.org
http://www.clm1.org

Institute for Supply Management
PO Box 22160
Tempe, AZ 85285-2160
800/888-6276
http://www.ism.ws

Textile Engineering

A major in textile engineering prepares students to work in a global industry that not only includes traditional apparel and home furnishing applications, but also cutting-edge applications in the plastics, packaging, biomedical, marine, construction, environmental, automotive, aerospace, industrial, safety, and other industries. Textile engineers draw on diverse science and engineering principles, and have an abundance of career opportunities available to them. Degrees in textile engineering are available at all academic levels.

Typical Courses:

> Calculus
> Chemistry
> Physics
> Yarn Engineering
> Weaving and Knitting; Nonwovens
> Polymer Synthesis and Processing
> Dyeing and Finishing
> Statistics
> Industrial Textiles
> Textile Production Control

Potential Employers:

> Chemical manufacturers
> Global textile retail companies
> Automotive companies
> Government forensic science agencies

Available At:

The following list of schools offering programs in textile engineering is not exhaustive. For more programs, visit http://www.abet.org/accrediteac.asp.

Auburn University
Department of Polymer and Fiber Engineering
115 Textile Engineering
Auburn, AL 36849-5327
334/844-4123

http://www.eng.auburn.edu/programs/txen/about/index.html
Degrees available: Bachelor's degree, master's degree, doctorate
degree

Clemson University
School of Materials Science and Engineering
160 Sirrine Hall
Clemson, SC 29634-0907
864/656-1512
http://mse.clemson.edu
Degrees available: Bachelor's degree, master's degree, doctorate
degree

Georgia Institute of Technology
The School of Polymer, Textile and Fiber Engineering
801 Ferst Drive, NW, MRDC 1
Atlanta, GA 30332-0295
404/894-2490
webadmin@ptfe.gatech.edu
http://www.ptfe.gatech.edu
Degrees available: Bachelor's degree, master's degree, doctorate
degree

North Carolina State University
College of Textiles
2401 Research Drive, Box 8301
Raleigh, NC 27695
919/515-6637
http://www.tx.ncsu.edu/departments/tecs/textile_engineer.html
Degrees available: Bachelor's degree, master's degree, doctorate
degree

Philadelphia University
School of Engineering and Textiles
School House Lane & Henry Avenue
Philadelphia, PA 19144-5497
215/951-2700
http://www.philau.edu/engineering/BStextileengineeringtech
Degrees available: Bachelor's degree, master's degree, doctorate
degree

For More Information:

American Apparel and Footwear Association
1601 North Kent Street, Suite 1200
Arlington, VA 22209
http://www.americanapparel.org

National Council of Textile Organizations
910 17th Street, NW, Suite 1020
Washington, DC 20006
202/822-8028
http://www.ncto.org

Interview: John Rust

Dr. John Rust is the Director of the Textile Engineering Program at North Carolina State University in Raleigh, North Carolina. He discussed the field with the editors of *They Teach That in College!?*

Q. Who is a textile engineer?

A. It's someone who, for example:
  ✓ Develops a nano-composite material for deep space exploration
  ✓ Integrates a worldwide distribution program, eliminating a company's reliance on regional stockpiles
  ✓ Develops new biocompatible materials for artificial organs, blood vessels, tendons, or ligaments
  ✓ Designs a tent capable of sensing chemical and biological warfare

281

Q. Please provide an overview of your program.

A. The Textile Engineering Program at North Carolina State University is administered jointly by the College of Textiles and the College of Engineering and is an interdisciplinary curriculum drawing on diverse science and engineering principles. Textile engineering students develop a unique background, which allows them to pursue undergraduate research, summer intern experiences, and design projects ranging from artificial blood vessel development to the design of novel high-tech sporting equipment. The program offers small class sizes with personal attention from faculty. In addition, in the last three years graduates have had nearly 100 percent placement into full time employment or graduate school. Compared to the rest of North Carolina State University, the College of Textiles has the highest percentage of students participating in its scholarship programs. Indeed, more than 50 percent of all Textile Engineering students receive scholarship support.

Q. What high school subjects/activities should students focus on to be successful in this major?

A. As with any other engineering major, mathematics, chemistry, and physics are very important. However, we also recognize the importance of our students being well-informed citizens, and so we encourage the arts, languages, and broad experiences in the classroom as well as in the community.

Q. What are the most important qualities for textile engineering majors?

A. Generally, we are seeking students who are interested in a challenge and improving the world around them. Important attributes include honesty and a desire to learn and grow within a nurturing environment.

Q. How will the field of textile engineering change in the future?

A. It's changing now and has been since inception. With the focus on interdisciplinary research, the future of textiles has never been brighter. Textile engineers teaming up with chemists, physicists, materials scientists, and other engineers are designing new polymers, fibers, and textile structures to revolutionize the future of materials. Whether it be for personal protective garments such as bullet proof vests and Goretex(R), or materials used in the next generation space shuttle and the stealth bomber (and everything in between), textile engineers are developing products that are stronger, lighter, and more durable than current materials and products used.

Toy Design

The business of toys is for the truly multitalented individual—serious and analytical on the one hand, and young-at-heart, carefree, and creative on the other. Toy design students must be technologically inclined and business minded as they study the manufacturing of plastic and non-plastic toys, computer-aided industrial design, safety and regulatory requirements, and elements of consumer motivation. Yet the successful toy designer must also be able to maintain the mindset of the ultimate consumer—the child. According to the Fashion Institute of Technology (one of only two toy design schools in the United States), graduates go on to become product managers, inventors, toy research and development specialists, and designers of plush toys, dolls, action figures, vehicles, games, construction sets, and other playthings.

Typical Courses:

> Soft Toy and Doll Design
> Drafting for Toy Design
> Product Materials and Safety Considerations
> Games
> Hard Toy: Engineering
> Model Making
> Interactive Media for Toy Design
> Marker Rendering
> Licensed Product Design
> Computer Graphics in Toy Design

Potential Employers:

> Toy manufacturers (such as Hasbro, Gund, Mattel/Fisher-Price, LucasArts, Lego, LeapFrog, Wild Planet, and VTech)

Did You Know?

The United States produced 41 percent of all toys (excluding video games) in the world in 2003, according to the International Council of Toy Industries.

Available At:

Fashion Institute of Technology
Toy Design Program
Seventh Avenue at 27th Street
New York, NY 10001-7665
212/217-7665
fitinto@fitnyc.edu
http://www.fitnyc.edu/aspx/Content.aspx?menu=Future:Schools
AndPrograms:ArtAndDesign:ToyDesign

Did You Know?

Tickle Me Elmo, Blue's Clues, Don't Spill the Beans, and Hot
Wheels were all designed by graduates from the Fashion
Institute of Technology's Toy Design program.

Degrees available: Bachelor's degree
Otis College of Art and Design
Toy Design Program
9045 Lincoln Boulevard
Los Angeles, CA 90045
310/665-6985
toydesign@otis.edu
http://www.otis.edu
Degrees available: Bachelor's degree

For More Information:

Industrial Designers Society of America
45195 Business Court, Suite 250
Dulles, VA 20166-6717
idsa@idsa.org
http://www.idsa.org

Toy Industry Association, Inc.
1115 Broadway, Suite 400
New York, NY 10010
info@toy-tia.org
http://www.toy-tia.org

Playthings Magazine
http://www.playthings.com

Travel Industry Management

Do you love traveling to exotic places? Do you enjoy planning every minute detail of a family vacation? Are you fascinated with the behind-the-scenes world of the travel industry? If so, here is the job for you! Career opportunities abound in travel management—one of the nation's largest industries. As a travel management professional, you'll be responsible for helping consumers get the most for their vacation dollars. You'll advise, coordinate and give alternatives for destinations, modes of travel, and accommodations. Programs, varying from certificate to a master's degree, stress business skills to prepare students for management positions throughout the travel industry. Practical work is also required with onsite experience in a variety of travel and tourism settings.

Typical Courses:

> Hotel and Restaurant Management
> Food and Beverage Management
> Travel Industry Marketing
> Destination Development and Marketing
> Managerial Economics
> Accounting
> Business Law
> Human Resource Management
> Travel Industry Financial Analysis and Controls
> Passenger Transportation Management

Potential Employers:

> Hotels
> Restaurants
> Airlines
> Cultural institutions
> Museums
> Convention bureaus
> Travel agencies
> Tour operators
> Consulting agencies
> Government agencies

Available At:

Arizona State University
Department of Recreation Tourism & Management
PO Box 37100
Mail Code 3251
Phoenix, AZ 85069-7100
602/543-6620
http://www.west.asu.edu/chs/RTM/index.htm
Degrees available: Bachelor's degree

College of DuPage
Travel and Tourism Program
425 Fawell Boulevard, IC 1031B
Glen Ellyn, IL 60137-6599
630/942-2556
http://www.cod.edu/academic/acadprog/occ_voc/Travel
Degrees available: Associate degree

Concord University
Marsh Hall 119, PO Box 1000
Athens, WV 24712-1000
304/384-5263
http://faculty.concord.edu/socsci/RTM/index.html
Degrees available: Bachelor's degree

Hawaii Pacific University
College of Business Administration
1164 Bishop Street
Honolulu, HI 96813
808/544-0283
businessadministration@hpu.edu
http://www.hpu.edu/index.cfm?section=undergrad36
Degrees available: Certificate, bachelor's degree, master's degree

Houston Community College-Central College
1300 Holman, PO Box 7849
Houston, TX 77270-7849
713/718-6072
http://ccollege.hccs.edu/workforc/hotel/travel/travel.htm
Degrees available: Certificate, associate degree

Miami Dade College (multiple campuses)
305/237-8888
mdccinfo@mdc.edu
https://sisvsr.mdc.edu/ps/sheet.aspx
Degrees available: Associate degree

Moraine Valley Community College
9000 West College Parkway
Palos Hills, IL 60465-0937
708/974-4300
Degrees available: Certificate, associate degree
http://www.morainevalley.edu

New York University
School of Continuing and Professional Studies
145 4th Avenue, Room 201
New York, NY 10003
212/998-7200
http://www.scps.nyu.edu/departments/degree.jsp?degId=13
Degrees available: Bachelor's degree, master's degree

Northern Virginia Community College (multiple campuses)
4001 Wakefield Chapel Road
Annandale, VA 22003-3796
703/323-3000
http://www.nv.cc.va.us/curcatalog/programs/tratou.htm
Degrees available: Associate degree

Rochester Institute of Technology
Department of Hospitality and Service Management
One Lomb Memorial Drive
Rochester, NY 14623-5603
585/475-2411
http://www.rit.edu/~932www/ugrad_bulletin/colleges/cast/
trmgmt.html
Degrees available: Bachelor's degree

For More Information:

National Tour Association
546 East Main Street
Lexington, KY 40508
859/226-4444, 800/682-8886
http://www.ntaonline.com

Outdoor Industry Association
4909 Pearl East Circle, Suite 200
Boulder, CO 80301
303/444-3353
info@outdoorindustry.org
http://www.outdoorindustry.org

Unity College

Unity College is a private, nonprofit college in Unity, Maine. It offers more environmental programs than any other college in the country, according to the U.S. Department of Education. Unity was founded in 1965 and is accredited by the New England Association of Schools and Colleges. Ninety percent of students receive financial aid; the average financial aid award is $10,272. The College has a student to faculty ratio of 13:1. Intercollegiate sports include basketball, soccer, and cross country for men and cross country, soccer, and volleyball for women. Unity awards associate and bachelor's degrees.

Available Fields of Study:

Associate Degrees
> Environmental Science
> Landscape Horticulture
> Liberal Studies

Bachelor's Degrees
> Adventure Education Leadership
> Adventure Therapy
> Aquaculture and Fisheries
> Conservation Law Enforcement
> Ecology
> Environmental Analysis
> Environmental Biology
> Environmental Education
> Environmental Humanities
> Environmental Policy
> Environmental Science
> Environmental Writing
> Forestry
> General Studies
> Landscape Horticulture
> Parks, Recreation, and Ecotourism
> Wildlife
> Wildlife Biology
> Wildlife Care and Education
> Wildlife Conservation

For More Information:

Unity College
PO Box 532
Unity, ME 04988
800/624-1024
admissions@unity.edu
http://www.unity.edu
Degrees available: Associate degree, bachelor's degree

Interview: Joe Saltalamachia

Unity College is a private, non-profit college in Unity, Maine. According to the U.S. Department of Education, Unity offers more environmental programs than any other college in the country. The editors of *They Teach That in College!?* spoke with Joe Saltalamachia, Associate Director of Admissions at Unity College, about this interesting college.

Q. Please describe Unity College in a few sentences.

A. Unity is an environmentally focused, liberal arts college. We have a strong connection to the environment while still providing a solid core for students to prepare them for "the real world."

Q. If you were asked to describe Unity students in three words, what would they be?

A. Unity Students are:
✓ Outdoorsy! Unity students are all outdoor oriented. Some are extreme, while others are just now discovering the outdoor world. They camp, hike, canoe, kayak, hunt, fish, bird watch, etc.-they do it all.
✓ Diverse. Our students are very diverse environmentally-tree huggers and tree cutters, deer hunters and animal rights activists, consumptive and non-consumptive users of our natural resources. You can find students who would be right at home in a safari club international meeting and others who would love to ride the waves aboard a Greenpeace ship. They are environmental, whether they embrace that word or not.

✓ Involved. Unity students get into what they are doing. They "walk the talk." They don't just talk about change, they do it. Whether it is getting involved in political conversation, doing community service, working to make Unity College a fully sustainable campus, or working to get the word out on bad environmental practices, our students don't just sit idly by. They go out and make change happen. They are the squeaky wheels!

Q. What type of academic background does the typical Unity student have?

A. Academically, the average student has a GPA of 3.0 and an SAT (when submitted) of 1040. Students range from the top 5 percent to the bottom third of their high school classes.

Q. Other than having an interest in the environment, what types of students are most successful at Unity?

A. Students who are willing to get involved in their education and take an interest, rather than just waiting for opportunity to come knocking, will be the most successful at Unity. We are very good at what we do, but we might be just another "environmental college" if our students didn't get involved. If a student is looking forward to a career and does nothing to help his or her cause, he or she might not be successful. I see the students who are involved and take an interest as our most successful.

Q. In terms of political beliefs, how would you describe Unity students?

A. We have students from the political right and the political left, but many in the center. Our goal is to get students to think 360 degrees around an environmental issue. They learn how to look at both sides, make an educated decision about the issue, and understand the point of the view of the other side. I would say that both sides (politically) are equally represented, but depending on the issue, you may find more support for one side or the other.

Q. Can you tell us about your freshmen orientation program?

A. The NOVA program is a week-long, wilderness-based orientation program required of all new students. It is an excellent way for students to get to know one another and learn more about Unity before they begin their freshman year.

Groups of 12 students (led by two group leaders) canoe, hike, kayak, orienteer, and perform community service, while at the same time learn about college policies, peer pressure (how to stay away from drug and alcohol abuse), how to make best use of their study time, and other issues that they will encounter as freshmen.

Each year we offer around five to six choices. Last year, we had a hiking trip in the 100-mile wilderness, an Appalachian trail hike, a sea kayaking trip on the Maine Island Trails, and two canoe trips to northern Maine. We had another hiking trip to the Bigelow Mountains and a base camp for students not confident enough to do the former.

Q. What are some of the most popular majors at Unity?

A. Conservation Law Enforcement is our most popular major. Unity is one of the only schools in the country offering a four-year degree in this field. Our second most popular major, Wildlife, has four distinct specialties: Wildlife Biology, Wildlife Care and Education, Wildlife Conservation, and Wildlife. Wildlife gives students more flexibility within the field and allows them to prepare for jobs that many would not consider to be wildlife related, like environmental consulting. Our third most popular major is Adventure Education Leadership. We also offer the only four-year degree in environmental writing in the United States. A Bachelor's of General Studies allows students to create their own major based on their individual environmental interests.

Q. What types of internship opportunities are available to students?

A. Internships are hands-on with federal and state government organizations, nonprofits, and private corporations. Most students are required to complete only one internship. However, students majoring in Wildlife Care and Education are required to do three internships. Students majoring in Environmental Biology or Wildlife Biology must complete a senior thesis instead of an internship, since this will better prepare them for graduate school.

Q. How do Unity graduates fare in the workforce?

A. Job placement for Unity graduates is very high, but we always tell students that the name of the college is not necessarily going to get you a job. How you sell yourself and what you have learned and retained is more important. Students should ask themselves the following questions: What type of person have I become in four years at Unity? Did I take advantage of the resources at Unity (such as lectures, hands-on work, field trips, clubs, internships, and summer experiences), or did I just go through the motions? Students that answer yes to these questions will find excellent employment opportunities.

Q. The general American public doesn't seem as aware of or as focused on environmental issues of late. How has that affected enrollment at Unity College?

A. Environmental issues are not in the forefront of public discussion as much as they were during the Clinton administration. This lack of publicity can hurt environmental colleges like Unity. Despite this, we had a record 168 freshmen in our entering class last year and enjoy strong retention of upper-level students. Environmental laws are still on the books and still have to be enforced, which means that there will always be a need for environmental workers. Unity students also tend to think outside the box and are taking advantage of those ideas to find and/or create employment. The field of ecotourism is growing and supplying many of our graduates with employment opportunities.

Wood Science and Technology

When most people think of forest products, they think of paper or the wood that is used to build furniture or construct houses. But there is a lot more to forest products than just paper and wood. Did you know that forest products, according to the Society of Wood Science and Technology, are used to create an anti-cancer drug, rayon clothing, molded panels in automobiles, vanilla flavoring in ice cream, and other products? *Wood science technology workers* study the physical, chemical, and biological properties of wood and the methods of growing and processing it for use in everyday life. To meet the growing demand for professionals in this industry, colleges and universities are offering undergraduate and graduate programs in wood science and technology—many of which are accredited by the Society of Wood Science and Technology.

Typical Classes:

> Introduction to Forest Biology
> Introduction to Forest Resources
> Introduction to Wood Science and Technology
> Wood Anatomy and Structure
> Physical and Mechanical Properties of Wood
> Wood Chemistry
> Adhesion and Adhesives Technology
> Harvesting Forest Products
> Wood Composites
> Wood Deterioration and Preservation
> Forest Products Business Management
> Forest Resource Economics

Potential Employers:

> Mills
> Manufacturers of wood products
> Wood suppliers
> Forest products associations
> Pulp and paper companies
> Government agencies
> Colleges and universities

Available At:

The following list of schools offering programs in wood science and technology is not exhaustive. For more programs, visit the Society of Wood Science and Technology's website, http://www.swst.org/schooldirectory.html.

University of Idaho
Department of Forest Products
PO Box 441132
Moscow, ID 83844-1132
forprod@uidaho.edu
http://www.cnrhome.uidaho.edu/forp
Degrees available: Bachelor's degree, master's degree, doctorate degree

University of Maine
Wood Science and Technology Program
5755 Nutting Hall
Orono, ME 04469-5755
800/WOOD-UNIV
woodscience@maine.edu
http://www.woodscience.umaine.edu
Degrees available: Bachelor's degree, master's degree, doctorate degree, graduate certificate

Did You Know?

Approximately 1.4 million people are employed in the U.S. forest products industry, according to the Society of Wood Science and Technology.

University of Minnesota
Department of Bio-based Products
Kaufert Lab
2004 Folwell Avenue
St. Paul, MN 55108-1305
shri.umn.edu
http://www.cnr.umn.edu/BP
Degrees available: Bachelor's degree, master's degree, doctorate degree

Mississippi State University
Department of Forest Products
PO Box 9820
Mississippi State, MS 39762-9820
612/624-1293
BioProducts@umn.edu
http://www.cfr.msstate.edu/forestp/fphome.htm
Degrees available: Bachelor's degree, master's degree, doctorate degree

State University of New York
Construction Management and Wood Products Engineering
1 Forestry Drive, 153 Baker Laboratory
Syracuse, NY 13210
315/470-6880
jabarton@esf.edu
http://www.esf.edu/wpe
Degrees available: Bachelor's degree, master's degree, doctorate degree

North Carolina State University
Wood Products Program
Box 8005
Raleigh, NC 27695-8005
http://www.ncsu.edu/wood
Degrees available: Bachelor's degree, master's degree, doctorate degree

Oregon State University
Wood Science and Engineering
119 Richardson Hall
Corvallis, OR 97331
woodscience@oregonstate.edu
http://woodscience.oregonstate.edu
Degrees available: Bachelor's degree, master's degree, doctorate degree

Pennsylvania State University
Wood Products Program
113 Ferguson Building
University Park, PA 16802
814/865-7541
ForestResources@psu.edu
http://www.sfr.cas.psu.edu/WoodProd/WoodProducts.html
Degrees available: Bachelor's degree, master's degree, doctorate degree

Virginia Polytechnic Institute and State University
Wood Science and Forest Products
230 Cheatham Hall, Mail Code 0323
Blacksburg, VA 24060
540/231-8853
vtwood@vt.edu
http://www.woodscience.vt.edu
Degrees available: Bachelor's degree, master's degree, doctorate
degree

West Virginia University
Wood Science and Technology
PO Box 6125
Morgantown, WV 26506-6125
http://www.forestry.caf.wvu.edu/wvu_woodscience
Degrees available: Bachelor's degree, master's degree, doctorate
degree

For More Information:

Society of Wood Science and Technology
One Gifford Pinchot Drive
Madison, WI 53726-2398
608/231-9347
vicki@swst.org
http://www.swst.org

School Index

301

Schools by State Index

Association/Organization Index

310

Also from College & Career Press!

College Spotlight newsletter!

"What college to choose and what programs to examine are topics that are increasingly complex for senior high school students. *College Spotlight* will help them and their counselors in a way that no other publication really does."
—*Essential Resources for Schools and Libraries,* March/April 2002

College Spotlight (ISSN 1525-4313) is a 12-page newsletter published in September, October, November, January, March, and May of each school year to help those concerned with selecting, applying to, evaluating, and entering college, as well as to provide other alternatives for today's high school graduates.

Each issue of *College Spotlight* offers:

✔ Fascinating and informative cover stories such as "Major revisions in store for the SAT" and "The forensic science major: so popular, it's a crime"

✔ Regular features, such as Free & Low-Cost Guidance Materials, Book Reviews, Financial Aid, and Diversity Issues (including stories such as "More minorities and women needed in computer science")

✔ Useful education statistics, surveys, and other interesting research

Read a sample issue and learn how to order by visiting www.collegeandcareerpress.com!

Subscription Rates:
1 year/$30 ($25 if payment accompanies your order)
2 years/$50 ($45 if payment accompanies your order)
3 years/$65 ($60 if payment accompanies your order)